CW01431464

Book cover by MRSS.

Edited by MRSS.

First edition 2024

# Dedication

This book is dedicated to my beloved Fiancé, Madelein. Meeting you was like stumbling upon a rare treasure in the vast sea of life. Our love story, woven with laughter, tears, and laughs - coupled with countless unforgettable moments - inspired the pages of this book.

Your unwavering support, boundless love, and endless encouragement have filled my life with meaning and joy. May our journey together continue to be as enchanting and beautiful as the story we envision.

With all my love,

Luke Berry

# MEETING MADELEIN

**Luke Berry**

AUTHOR | ENTREPRENEUR | VISIONARY

# Acknowledgements

I am profoundly grateful to my family for their unwavering support and encouragement throughout this journey. Your love and belief in me have been my guiding light.

To my friends, both old and new, thank you for standing by my side through thick and thin. Your presence in my life brings me endless joy and inspiration.

To my day ones, you know who you are. Your friendship and loyalty have been a constant source of strength and laughter.

I extend my heartfelt gratitude to my film crew, who captured the moments of my journey on reality television. Your professionalism and talent brought our story to life on screen.

Mackenzie, your editing helped clearly capture the beauty and vigor of our love and of Colombian culture alike. Albeit being tested, your graphic design skills helped showcase Madelein in such a regal and powerful light. Thank you.

Lastly, to my present and future fans, thank you for embracing my story with open hearts and minds. Your support means the world to me, and I am forever grateful for your enthusiasm and love.

# Table of Contents

# Introduction

How far would you go for love?

It all started as an adventure. My friends and I were seeking a new experience and felt Colombia was the place to go. Little did I know this trip would change my life forever.

I have always been willing to see the world and all it has to offer. What I was never prepared for was Madelein. I like to think that I am knowledgeable in the ways of women. You know, I've had a fair share of experiences with them. I was no novice in the matters of relationships, but was I ready for real love before meeting Madelein?

Maybe I imagined some idea of what love was about, but love was just a word before I met Madelein. I spent most of my life trying to find new encounters. New experiences. New hope.

It seemed like everything I ever was wasn't enough to justify my place in the universe. I have always wanted more from life, but I never knew in what direction or where I was going at all.

Without focus, speed is a waste of time. How does one know what to focus on? Who would have thought that love could transcend a vacation fling?

My world turned upside down but simultaneously felt right side up. All I wanted was to be by her side. My goals were shifting before my eyes, yet she remained consistent in my vision.

This story is about love and loss. It's about decisions birthed in the fire. It's about finding myself. It's about friendship. The gift of genuine connection. It's about risk. After all, what is life without a little risk? Or a lot?

I've come a long way in search of an elusive dream. With Madelein, I know I'm closer to the mark.

Love is everything they say it is and more. But what no one tells you is that love is labor. The labor to make something nonexistent into a reality. The labor to define yourself against all odds. There is a kind of love that grows in all of us. That is the kind I found in her.

What does the future hold? I'll tell you - something glorious. Grab a cookie or your favorite snack. Grab a glass of wine, an ice-cold beer, or the best drink you have. Relax. Get comfortable. Dive into my story, journey with me, and bear witness to one of the greatest love stories ever told.

# Searching For Love

## Chapter One

I was born in 1993 in Santa Monica, California. I am a first-generation American; my dad is British, and my mom is Mexican. A formidable combination if you ask me. Big soccer countries, which might have been the only thing they had in common.

I grew up in a household that reflected my diverse heritage—a blend of British reserve and Mexican warmth. My parents' contrasting backgrounds often played out in amusing ways, especially during soccer matches where they passionately supported their respective national teams. Despite their differences, they found common ground in their love for the game, which shaped much of our family life.

The naming saga that surrounded my birth was a testament to their unique partnership. Born in Santa Monica, California in 1993, I entered the world amidst a debate over what to call me. It took my parents two weeks to settle on "Luke," a name suggested by a nurse who confidently declared it to be the best option from a list. This decision was perhaps influenced by their earlier misadventure with my would-be name, "Meghan," which had been prematurely immortalized in concrete at our home. It became a humorous family anecdote, underscoring my parents' knack for blending seriousness with levity.

In contrast, my younger sister's name was chosen well in advance, a lesson learned from my unconventional naming process. Growing up with a sister who had a name prepared before birth brought a sense of stability and foresight that was missing from my own naming tale. Despite the initial uncertainty, the name "Luke" eventually grew into a perfect fit, embodying aspects of both my British and Mexican heritage—a subtle reminder of the diverse cultural tapestry that shaped my identity from the very beginning.

It took my parents two weeks to decide what I'd be named. They didn't have a gender reveal before my birth but believed wholeheartedly that I would have been a girl. So much so that they poured a concrete patch at the house with the name "Meghan" etched on it. The nurse gave my mom a list of names and told her Luke was the best one. That's how I got my name. They learned their lesson and picked my sister's name in advance.

My mom thought it was a good idea to grow my hair out until I was five years old. That's typically the time kids start preschool in the United States (U.S.), so when I went to school, I got made fun of and called a girl. Ironic, right?

My school was called Morning Glory and was in Venice, on Lincoln and Washington. It was a cool school. Shit, we had the time of our lives, taking naps and playing with toys. After Morning Glory, I went to a K-8 Catholic school called Saint Mark's Catholic School, also on Lincoln Blvd. in Venice. There were about 30 students in each class, so it was a close-knit student body. Everyone knew everyone, from their siblings to their extended families.

These were seriously some of the best days of my life. The good old days, when we were the cool kids on the block. Since there weren't that many kids, everyone got to know each other well, and the families would engage together. It came with its own consequences, though, like when we would all get in trouble together. Sometimes, we would hang out with the public school kids because we thought they were so much cooler than the private school kids. The private school parents didn't like that very much.

Another childhood memory I have is crushing on my second-grade teacher, who looked like Britney Spears. I swear - she looked like the Britney Spears album cover… At least she did to me at the time. I didn't *really* find interest in girls until later, like the fifth grade or so. I had a crush on a chick named Avery, who ended up being my first Valentine, but we were just kids and didn't do anything more than play dates.

I kissed an eighth-grade girl - as a sixth grader - who had a cousin in my sister's class named Robert. Robert had - and still has - the biggest crush on my sister. He used to fear me in elementary school and would run around the yard in the opposite direction as me. In seventh grade, I started dating our Vice Principal's niece. We got caught making out in the bathroom a couple of times, so my time at school was made somewhat difficult. I was a great student, though, and an awesome athlete, so they couldn't really do shit.

One time, in seventh grade, this kid in our class brought a PSP to school when they had just come out. He logged onto the school network and was looking at photos of women online. He was a sly cat and had concealed the PSP in a pencil bag, and passed it around to all the boys in class. Somehow, one of the girls saw - was obviously disturbed - and ratted on us. The teacher wasn't thrilled; we all got suspended.

I went through a lot of big changes in seventh grade. The controversial event featuring the PSP, a brand-new gadget, was the start of it all. One brave friend was able to connect it to the school network and sneakily look at some questionable online material. In our group of boys, the PSP was kept in a pencil case and passed from person to person until one of the girls found out about it. After she told the teacher about her shock, things went quickly from bad to worse—we were all suspended.

The problems that happened after that event were just the start of many changes in my life that year. Not long after what happened with the PSP, my parents said they were splitting up. Their choice shook my world in ways I didn't fully understand at the time. I had a hard time dealing with the mental turmoil that came with their breakup. I had no idea what the future held. My younger sister looked to me for security while my mother dealt with the upheaval in her marriage. This made me very aware of my place in the family.

It was hard for me to keep things normal in other parts of my life, like my relationships, while I was going through these personal problems. I was seeing the niece of the vice principal, which seemed to come with its own set of problems and demands. As the school year came to a close, I had to make the hard choice to end things because I couldn't handle the stress of a relationship while my family was having problems.

Later that year, my parents separated, and my life changed pretty drastically. In my eyes, there was some unshakable tenacity to their presence in my life. I was too young to navigate my feelings around the separation. I had a sister who looked up to me and a mother whose world had been shaken. I couldn't handle having a girlfriend, so I broke up with the Vice Principal's niece towards the end of that school year and then made my way into eighth grade.

I dated a bombshell from another school, who ended up becoming my high school sweetheart. We dated on-and-off throughout high school. I went to an all-boys Jesuit prep school called Loyola High. I graduated in 2011 and then went to college at the University of Arizona.

College is great, but the U of A is amazing - BTFD! I earned two bachelor's degrees, one in mining engineering and the other in geology.

As a sophomore in college, I lived in the TKE frat house on the second floor, overlooking the courtyard. Fraternity houses were a place of parties, women, and bro shit. It was so fun but was definitely a huge distraction from school.

Our parties were epic. The courtyard was where most people got down, but my roommate Bryan and I had a bar in our living room. It was an exclusive access, all-you-can-drink corner bar in our apartment living room. We would have parties in our room. Some for the record books. We were well-versed on partying, and the girls were another animal.

Having realized that young love was mostly a ruse, I began to weave my path through the hearts of several girls. I didn't commit myself to anyone and was single most of college until the later years.

I joined a Collegiate Mining Competition team at my school for a couple of years. They have an annual competition, but the location is different each time - so some destinations are better than others. It was announced my year would compete in Australia right around spring break. I did the only logical thing and took off one week before spring break to Australia. I spent 21 total days there and had the time of my life. Australian women are awesome, and they absolutely love Americans. Supposedly the Aussie boys are shit, so taking their girls was funny.

I met this girl, Maddie, who went to Berkeley after getting back from Australia. We hit it off and ended up dating for five years. For the first time in a long while, I put a stop to the other ladies and focused on her, but life after college was not what it was cracked up to be.

I got my first job in no-man's land - Boron, CA. The excitement of a job was interesting for a while, but I must confess, nothing prepares you for a 1-hour daily commute to and from work. I moved to Lancaster and commuted every day to Boron for a year and a half. My body slowly drained and revolted, so I had to ask myself if I had the guts to continue that rat race. I went back to Los Angeles every weekend because Lancaster sucked. It got to the point that, eventually, I took a job in aggregates; I switched from mining specialty minerals to rock and sand for construction materials, a completely different sector in the mining industry, and moved back to Los Angeles!

I started work as a Project Engineer in LA and was quickly promoted within the company. They moved me down to San Diego and gave me a Production Manager role at a site in Miramar. I was promoted again and became an Area Operations Manager, with a higher salary allowed me to buy a house. While I was managing 6 business lines, I went back to school to earn my MBA in Location Analytics.

After getting my master's degree, I entered a sales role and worked in a hybrid-remote setting. My house in San Diego had an ADU that brought in $1,700/month in rental income while I had been living in the main 3 bed/2 bath house. I thought it would be in my best interest to rent out the main house for extra income and move back in with my mom in LA. We converted the back garage into a bachelor pad for me so I could have a little bit of privacy as a grown adult.

Life was good, money was great, but during this time, I was in and out of relationships. Nothing about my love life really seemed to be working out for me.

Remember Avery from the sixth grade? Well, it turns out she had a younger sister who fancied me. We dated for a while during COVID, but it didn't work out in the end.

Following that relationship, one of my best friends, Diego, planned a Tahoe getaway for his girlfriend's birthday party. Diego and his girlfriend (Chelsea), my other best friend (Alejandro) and his girlfriend (Alexa) and Chelsea's friend (Katie) were all in attendance for the trip. Basically, rebounding with each other from past relationships, Katie and I hooked up there and dated for a bit afterward. A year later, I went to surprise her at her apartment, only to be surprised myself when I walked in on her cuddling with her ex. Super weird experience. She yelled, and I got out.

My dumbass didn't think they were hooking up, either. How can emotions be so blinding? Anyhow, the fallout from that relationship was exponential. It went from bad to worse.

I sought a therapist for a while to release my mind from the whole affair. From there, I joined a mental toughness program geared towards getting back on track. The kicker was this particular toughness program required no drinking.

So here I am at the bar with Robert - the guy in my sister's class that had a crush on her - talking about starting this challenge when it dawned on us what this challenge entailed. For 75 days, you could not drink, had to follow a diet, drink a gallon of water, read 10 pages of a professional development book, and take progress photos. Andy Frisela is a beast of an entrepreneur and came up with it. I was a huge fan of his podcast and figured, "What the hell? It should only help us, and we get the added benefits of getting back in shape."

Robert was hitting on the bartender, and then the guy next to us told us she's his girlfriend. This guy was from Colombia and told us:

**Bar Guy:** The finest women in the world are from Medellin!

To this, Robert quickly followed with:

**Robert:** Let's go there after our 75 Hard Challenge!

That's how I was roped into going to Colombia. Poised and excited for Colombia, we started 75 Hard the very next day.

# Landing in Colombia

## Chapter Two

Columbia seemed like a breath of fresh air for my much-needed recovery. My friends and I were pumped for the experience. After all, what could go wrong in a city that held so much promise for adventure? I was looking good and feeling super positive about everything happening in my life.

I had always been enthralled by the boisterous disposition of South Americans. The vivacity in which they approached life and their never-ending zest for fun. The promise of beautiful women. The longing for endless binging on margaritas also titillated my senses. There was so much to venture out for.

I needed to permanently shut off the previous heartbreak and forge a new path away from that memory. Colombia just seemed like the right place to be. I had always been eager to see the place where the famed Pablo Escobar was able to wield so much influence. Or Shakira even. I idolized both people for different reasons. Little did I know, I would model some travel packages for my future business after both iconic individuals.

One morning, during the mental toughness program, just after getting back from one of my morning jogs to the beach, a certain yearning gripped my mind. I don't know how the thought tugged at my heart for so long, until it became a loud voice nudging me towards an adventure. That was when I knew, there and then, that going to Colombia was more than a desire. It had become a lifeline out of the doldrums.

I buzzed up a buddy from way back, Nico, with whom we played soccer together back in our school days. He was from Ecuador. A solid dude. We kept in touch even after not seeing each other. He was one of those people who was always looking for something out there. There was always some better place to be. He had stayed in Colombia some years back, so it just made sense that I consult his counsel before the trip. He connected me with his buddy Daniel. Daniel had gone to school in Culver City with Nico and had moved to Colombia. He was going to be the local plug while we were there.

I called Robert and Zach and scheduled a date for our trip, which was September 2nd. What remained undecided was how long we intended to stay, but I packed enough to last me a month.

Next was our itinerary. What and where did we intend to visit? Meanwhile, our list on Tinder began to pile up. Robert was already thinking of a spacious Airbnb to accommodate the litany of ladies. As for Zach, he was more concerned about what Colombia looked like. He had his sight set on the Pablo Escobar crash site.

We wanted to see Medellin, since we remembered what the guy at the bar said. Nico had convinced us to visit Cartagena as well. Medellin was supposed to be the hustle and bustle city and nightlife that everyone talked about, so we couldn't miss that. Cartagena had the beachy party vibes that we also wanted to experience. We booked some super dope Airbnb's and browsed some excursions. Robert was extra excited because of all the pretty girls he saw on Tinder. Zach was stoked to get out of the States. I was pumped for a new cultural experience.

Leading up to the trip, I was on Tinder and matched with pretty women, but had fallen head over heels for one, who I met on Instagram. Her name was Madelein, and she was in Medellin. As far as I was concerned, I just wanted to meet her when I was in Medellin. Anything else was fine with me. This trip was going to be awesome, and I couldn't wait.

With each passing hour, I realized that Madelein's stories about Medellin, with its lively dance clubs, busy markets, and beautiful views from the mountains that surround it, were becoming more and more appealing to me. As our online relationship grew stronger, each message and picture we sent each other made me look forward to our next meeting even more. I was excited about the next journey. Even though they made fun of me the whole time, I didn't mind that my friends teased me for being interested. Beyond just a place, Medellin had become connected with the hope of meeting someone very important.

The flight to Colombia was long and quite interesting. Zach and Robert managed to get seats close to each other, while I shared my space with a war veteran who was going back home for the first time in 20 years. His only daughter had been put to bed, and his wife had passed on the previous year, so he wanted to fill that void for his daughter. He missed his wife. I did not remember to ask his age, but he seemed like a man in his 70s. Clean-shaven, with a rosary around his neck. He was wearing a flannel shirt with blue jeans. His palm was tough, and his grip even stronger.

At some point in our discussion, he asked:

**War Veteran:** What's your deal in Colombia?

**Luke:** I dunno. Just some sightseeing and introspection.

He smiled as I said that, and I could see the crinkle at the corner of his eyes.

**War Veteran**: Introspection is good, you know, with the way your generation seems to move with the trends. You'd wonder if any of you thought of your futures instead of fantasizing over Latina women!

**Luke:** It all depends. Most times, we prefer not to wear our hearts on our sleeves.

He smiled again. A bit broader this time, and I could see some brown spots around his premolars. Probably tobacco, but our conversation was more pressing than whatever the color of his teeth looked like.

At some point in the journey, Robert would twitch in his seat and turn his head backward. He could not understand how I wasn't paying attention to whatever it was he and Zach were engaged in. For all it was worth, I was enjoying the company of the old man.

When the announcement came on from the cockpit, my heart began to beat faster. For some reason, it seemed like there was so little time to catch up with the country and so many places to see. I had told Daniel to expect us, but we never really settled on where to meet when we landed.

Rob traveled light. Just a backpack. I had two bags with me - I didn't want to take chances. Zach seemed to share each of our sentiments, traveling with a backpack and a duffel bag.

The air in Colombia was inviting. Misty with a sweet smell. The boys and I could not wait to plunge into the heart of Columbia. I called Daniel but couldn't connect with him. His phone was off, and for some reason, a tinge of disappointment flashed through my mind. As I dropped the call, a notification beeped from Airbnb that the place we had booked was unavailable due to a gas leak at the apartment, three days prior to our coming. It's a wonder it took them three days to notify us. It could have been fixed, but for some reason, they didn't see the urgency. This was a dent to our collective enthusiasm.

I had to rally the boys, and we began to brainstorm for alternatives. We searched for another available Airbnb. We couldn't find the kind we wanted, so we opted for a hotel. Our taxi guy seemed to have a lot of suggestions on where he thought would best fit us.

**Taxi Driver:** I know a hotel where Americans like to stay.

He was struggling hard to sound more Northern than us. Robert and Zach gave me the side eye, the three of us chuckled, and then Rob blurted:

**Rob:** If there are humans there and it's not some cheap-ass lodge, get us someplace reasonable!

His comment eased the stress, and as the taxi drove through the busy streets of Colombia, we all laughed. Even though the taxi driver's idea caused a small problem, we weren't going to let it ruin our excitement about being in a new country.

Just getting to Colombia felt like a victory in and of itself. We were tired from the long trip, but now we were ready to see more and enjoy our time. I looked over at Robert's phone and saw him swiping left and right on Tinder. This made me think of what we had talked about earlier, how we wanted to meet new people and maybe make connections during our stay.

From the taxi window, we could see and hear the lively sights and sounds of Colombia, which made us look forward to our travels. We were ready to enjoy every moment of our trip to Colombia, whether it was figuring out subtle cultural differences, meeting friendly locals like our car driver, or just enjoying the thrill of being somewhere new.

We had gotten to Colombia, and that was all that mattered. We weren't going to allow a temporary setback to ruin our plans. I looked over Robert's phone as the car rode on, and I could see his fingers swiping left and right on Tinder.

# Meeting Madelein

## Chapter Three

***

Hotel Salmon towered and loomed largely over the city of Medellin. Just before our taxi driver dropped us off, he gave us some directions. Albeit unsolicited, they were quite useful in a sense. As we said goodbye and thank you, he said:

**Taxi Driver:** Stay invisible.

To me, it seemed he was either truly concerned or trying so hard to make us feel like we were in a new terrain.

**Robert:** Do you see Zach here?

I said this jokingly, gesturing to measure Zach's height and width.

**Robert:** His presence is enough to scare off any criminal mind!

The taxi driver laughed and waved off my gestures, turned on the ignition, and drove away.

As I watched his taillights trail off, I wondered how skepticism seemed to have slowly warmed itself into the hearts of men and how we had to be extra conscious towards everything. There was a time when one would have relished going to a foreign land without having to ponder so much on one's security. We were three men with imposing figures - it was quite difficult to remain invisible.

Hotel Salmon was a sprawling white structure standing 24 stories tall. As we sauntered towards the reception, it was evident that the typical needs of a tourist were well-catered to. You could see foreigners muttering English, which seemed like a decent sign. There was a line of female receptionists, who looked like they were carved out of the finest wood - which Robert nudged my side to get my attention about. Zach was already taking mental notes of what to say when we were called next. None of us were fluent in Spanish.

**Robert:** I'll take the one on row three, that blonde one.

It was the typical Robert act - always quick to pick out the ladies from the crowd.

I spoke to the receptionist and reserved two rooms. Zach and Robert shared a room while I was hoping to bring Madelein back to mine. I sent her a text to see where she was, thinking I was so slick:

**Luke:** Hola mamacita, ¿dóndeestás?

She responded by inviting us to Provenza, an outside promenade full of restaurants and discotheques. She cruised over to the hotel to meet up with us before dinner. Daniel came through with party supplies, and from there, we were ready to go. Our cab to Provenza was super small. The cab driver complained I shut the door too forcefully when Madelein explained that car doors in Colombia have less insulation, I needed to be careful. Oooops.

We had already corresponded with some of the ladies on Tinder, and Robert tried to score a date with someone for our group dinner. No bites yet.

We went to a restaurant on the corner of one of the most vibrant streets in Provenza called Chef's Burger. They sat us at an upstairs bar and brought us margaritas right away - total vibe. They even brought out a frozen watermelon dish that Madelein was in love with.

The refreshing sweetness of the watermelon was a perfect complement to the warm evening, and it quickly became a favorite among our group. As we enjoyed our meal, we couldn't help but notice the eclectic mix of people around us - from trendy locals to curious tourists, all drawn to Provenza's reputation as a hub of culture and nightlife.

Provenza is a crazy place in Medellin where the ratio of women to men is insane. There are probably 9 to 11 girls for every guy. The vibrant streets of Provenza seemed to pulse with energy, lined with colorful buildings housing hip cafes, stylish boutiques, and bustling bars. It was a scene that captivated our senses and sparked our curiosity, prompting us to explore every corner and soak in the unique atmosphere. Robert and Zach were in Heaven. After dinner, Madelein invited us to go to the discotheque.

We started at Club 818, which was a world of its own. It was nothing like what I was used to in Los Angeles. The music had amazing vibes, and the drinks were so cheap. The more I drank, the more I thought to myself that I had never seen a woman more beautiful in all my life.

She let her hair loose over her shoulders. She was wearing a beige Burberry skirt that accentuated her hips and matching crop top. One of the appeals that she evoked in me was her ability to carry herself with so much grace. She walked like the Earth was a delicate place to trample upon. She was such a good dancer, too. She moved those hips like Shakira and had a nice, slim, gorgeous body.

We got a bottle of Don Julio and a bunch of water bottles. We started becoming comfortable in conversation, to say the least.

**Madelein:** What do you think of Colombia?

**Luke:** Well, I just got here some hours ago; ask me in a couple of days.

We both smiled. She brought out some pills from her bag and slipped two into her mouth.

**Luke:** What are those? precaution pills?

She moved her head side to side and let out a deep laugh.

**Madelein:** Luke, you aren't getting any ideas, right? Here, have some.

She beckoned on me to open my mouth, and I did, while she slipped a pill into it.

**Madelein:** This is just a little something to get the night going.

In a few seconds, I began to feel my mind being lifted out of my body. My head was swooning, and I began to see myself as an actor in a major movie, even though Madelein was proving to be quite popular within the club. Friends would come to our space to hug her. At some point, I felt intimidated knowing that she knew this many people and so well-known. But the pills were kicking in, and my inhibitions were frayed.

We danced. She had a way with movements, like she was born in a dance school. She told me she won a salsa dancing competition when she was younger; I was super impressed and got some thoughts about what it would be like if it were just her and I alone in a room together, but eventually, it was difficult to keep up with her pace.

She slipped a second pill into my mouth, and this time, I began to move with more efficiency. It wasn't long before I realized I not only needed a drink but also forgot about the boys. I went to the table they were at and had a drink from the tequila bottle we ordered. When I went back to the dancefloor, I realized next - I had lost Madelein.

I have a thing for big butts - and I cannot lie! I saw a chick twerking next to me, wanting to dance, so I started grinding on her. I might have gotten carried away, which I realized by the look on Madelein's face when I turned to look for her again. By then, we seemed to have a connection and Madelein was clearly jealous. I was caught off guard and didn't know what to do, so I did the only logical thing in the moment - and looked in another direction. A couple of moments later, I slipped away as the crowd began to jump in vibrating synchronicity to a song by Pitbull.

I looked around, hoping to find Madelein, but instead saw Robert making out with some girl on the dance floor. She was giggling and wildin'. I gave him a thumbs up and resumed my search for Madelein. A waiter brought her bag to me, and I hung it on my shoulders as I meandered through a stream of bodies. I found Zach sitting in a corner with two chicks. He looked exhausted. I looked at my watch, and it was 2 am. I went to our table and took two more tequila shots - which was also the last thing I remembered at Club 818.

It wasn't until some minutes past 10 am that the buzzing of the phone roused me from my sleep. My head was heavy, while the vigorous hangover - of a hammer hitting ice - was telling on me for last night's decisions. I dragged myself towards the ringing phone and picked-up:

**Receptionist:** Sir, Madelein is here to see you. Should I let her into your suite?

That was when it dawned on me. I had been with Madelein the previous night. It all came back at once. The other chick was twerking on me. The pills. I was trying too hard to recall every detail. I didn't want to face Madelein, having not known what excesses I may have indulged in.

**Luke:** Let her in.

What was the worst that could happen? After all, she was partly responsible. Those pills were something else. She came into my room, and I offered her some coffee, which she declined.

**Madelein:** You look like you need more of that than I do.

She chuckled. That was something about Madelein that made my heart flutter. Her smile. The ability for her to lose herself with grace. I smiled wanly.

**Madelein:** Do you perhaps have my bag?

Before I could say yes, she moved over to the side of my bed and picked up a purple bag from the floor.

**Madelein:** Aren't I lucky?

She smiled. I couldn't help but ask:

**Luke:** When will I see you again?

**Madelein:** It's up to you to decide, but I must go now. Enjoy the city.

I half hoped she was interested in me. From our interactions, I saw that she found it easy to get along with anyone without trying so hard. There wasn't any hint of me being anything special. It just seemed like a natural thing to relate with courtesy.

The boys and I decided to get some breakfast. Robert had come back to his room with the girl from the previous night, and the four of us had breakfast at The Ravens Cafe. I had an omelet with a slice of buttered bread and hot coffee. I felt some relief in my head.

**Zach:** While you were snoring your ass out, we took the liberty of searching for a new Airbnb in Poblado.

I was grateful for their thoughtfulness. I texted Madelein when we finished eating. I was feeling bored and in need of company - but also, did I fuck things up with her?

We still had some hours left for our hotel reservations before checking out. Robert was still with "his guest" and paid little attention to us. As for Zach, he was busy looking for the dopiest spots for us to visit. We were in one of the coolest cities in the world, after all.

At the hotel, we were approached by a tour guide who was promoting a vibrant part of Medellin known for artistic expressions.

**Tour Guide:** Comuna 13 is a place that has historical significance and represents a place of rebirth.

Who knew graffiti art could be so deep? We were sold.

**Luke:** When do you leave?

**Tour Guide:** Dos Horas.

We went on a walk in the park to kill some time. There were all kinds of tropical flowers splattered across the park. Just across the park, I saw Madelein in the company of a guy. He wore a leather jacket and a white round-neck shirt. She was wearing a flowery gown. I thought to myself, is that her? Am I seeing things? My initial impulse was to confront her, but I thought against it. I had barely met her. Maybe she decided against seeing me since I embarrassed her at the discotheque last night. Maybe I wasn't the person she expected me to be. Lots of "buts" and "maybes" crept through my mind. They were walking towards us.

I turned away from their direction and looked at my wristwatch. I looked up as they were nearer, and to my surprise, it wasn't her. This girl wasn't the petite Madelein from the night before. I was relieved.

Robert, Zach, and I met up with the tour group and went over to Comuna 13. The pueblo had a lot of character and tons of street vendors. Everything was painted in pastel colors and was covered with vibrant murals. The murals told the story of the transition of the town and how they combatted violence. I loved hearing the history behind it.

We stopped at a bar to grab a couple of Micheladas. Karol G music started playing, and then a swarm of people gathered outside the bar. People started dancing and rapping - what a spectacle.

**Zach:** Colombia is lit!

We all agreed.

The graffiti tour finished early, and Zach had planned a boys' day trip to Guatape for the next day.

**Zach:** We should get an early night, boys, just in case.

So, of course, we went to a bar. A couple of drinks later, and I was beginning to itch for some company. In all my travels, I had always explored with the women of the city. I needed to see who they were and what they were all about. Madelein wasn't with us, unfortunately, but there were many more fish in the sea.

At the bar, I ordered a beer. I normally drink IPAs, but few places in Medellin had them. I got a Corona instead, and it tasted good. So, I ordered three more bottles.

**Isabella:** Are you in need of some company?

She looked like a light-skinned, porcelain doll. She had a nose ring and a short skirt that revealed her long, soft legs. Her blonde hair was rolled up into a bun, and she had quite a large buxom. Maybe it was the beer speaking, but at that moment, I wasn't thinking about Madelein.

**Luke:** Well, it depends on the company.

I didn't want to seem desperate. Besides, I had never been one to lack the attraction of women. It wasn't a big deal that we were having that conversation. If anything, I saw her as an experience in transit.

**Luke:** My name is Luke. ¿Quieres una cerveza?

She smiled.

**Isabella:** And I thought for a moment you were playing hard to get.

**Luke:** Not really; I don't play games.

**Isabella:** Do we have trust issues now?

I could see her dimples. She was beautiful, yet rough around the edges. She chewed on gum carelessly, like she wasn't concerned about the effect on others.

**Isabella:** Are you on vacation? A job or whatever?

I didn't like the idea of being interviewed by a stranger whom I had barely known. Especially one who was giving the green light. Was she baiting me? Anyways, the beer was lowering my resolve, so I felt it wasn't necessary if she knew some bits of me. Besides, I didn't see her as some long-term plan.

The waiter delivered her cocktail, so I asked:

**Luke:** What are your plans tonight?

I could see her flirting with the bar attendant. I guess they had some history.

**Luke:** I haven't gotten your name yet.

**Isabella:** It's Isabella.

She smiled, and I could see those dimples again. She placed her hands on my thighs and caressed me with steady precision.

**Isabella:** Can we go to your hotel?

It was a huge turn-off for me. I didn't like the idea of her hitting on me like that. It made me feel like I was being baited, but maybe I was feeling insecure. I really can't say.

**Luke:** Patience, chica.

**Isabella:** Fair enough.

Robert and Zach approached and said they were headed back to the crib. I was tipsy and wanted to stay.

Isabella and I went to Club 818, and by that time, it was 12 am, and the stars were glittering in the sky. Isabella turned out to be quite an intense person. She swayed her hips like she had no bones. Moved her arms like an enchantress. Swung her heart from side to side like Shakira did in a music video capable of unraveling at any minute. She held me, spellbound with her moves, and I forgot about everything - keeping my gaze on her.

We danced, and as our bodies brushed against themselves, I could feel my heart burning with desire. We had gotten so engrossed in ourselves that we could barely get our hands off each other. And then a hand tapped on my shoulders. Next thing I see is a straight punch on my chin. It hurt like hell.

I regained my composure and saw three guys. One was holding a knife, and the other two had this menacing look on their faces.

**Guy with Knife:** What are you doing with my girl?

**Luke:** Your girl? Dude, I barely knew her; we were just having a dance.

Isabella's head was bowed. One of the guys held tightly to her hand.

**Luke:** I am sorry dude. I didn't know who she was.

Almost simultaneously, I heard Madelein's voice from behind me.

**Madelein:** He's with me.

Relief and angst danced within my belly. The guys backed out and took Isabella away with them.

**Madelein:** Welcome to Colombia.

She smiled, and I didn't know what to make of it. I was embarrassed that she had to find me in that position.

**Luke:** I guess it wouldn't be out of place to call you my guardian angel.

Again, she smiled, and again, my heart melted into a thousand directions. She took my hands and led me to the bar. Got some ice and placed it on my chin. It didn't hurt like it did some minutes earlier, and her presence seemed to have a soothing effect.

**Luke:** Thanks, Madelein.

**Madelein:** I saw you at Comuna 13 today, Luke.

I felt goosebumps on my body. Here I was, thinking I was the only one who saw her, not knowing she also had seen me.

**Madelein:** I know you may be wondering why I didn't respond. Truth is, I had to go help my grandma with something.

I didn't know what to say other than:

**Luke:** All good.

I was trying to remember what happened, and I didn't want to embarrass myself any more than I already had. She was super understanding and got me a cab back home.

The guys didn't even make a fuss when I got back to our spot. Robert had barely left his room. Zach was on his laptop watching a new episode from his favorite television series. I was beginning to think that Colombia was another planet, and I was far away from reality. I lay on my bed and thought of Madelein. Her eyes looked like they were calling my soul towards a cause. Her voice sounded like a sweet melody. If she were eager to talk about what happened tonight, then maybe there was some spark there.

I went to the bathroom and took a shower. I ran my fingers through my hair and touched my chin - it ached slightly. I wondered what might be happening to Isabella right now. How did she get herself in such company? Was it pure luck that Madelein was there to rescue me?

I lay back on the bed, and the next thing I heard was a tap on the door and the voices of my friends.

**Rob:** Luke, get your ass up, we leave in one hour.

Oh, so Rob is back from oblivion, I thought to myself.

**Luke:** Shut up, dude. I thought you were stuck with some titties in your face.

We all laughed. I had missed hanging out with the boys. The time was 7:45 am. I hopped out of bed and gathered the bits of my stuff that I had brought out of my bag. I was a bit tired but ready for the boys' day.

28

# The Adventures of Guatape

## Chapter Four

Z ach had marked Guatape as the boys' trip destination, which would require a 2-hour bus ride to get there. Having secured our new Airbnb prior, the boys didn't have to stress, and it was time to focus on vacation. Next was itinerary-building-time on the boys' day Zach planned. I had missed the company of the boys, and I desperately wanted us to kick-start our adventure in full swing. Robert's girl, that he was hanging out with had fallen out. I guess it was one of the reasons he was so eager to get going, but I didn't really care for the details.

As we boarded the bus, the excitement was palpable. The rolling landscape of Colombia unfolded before us, a tapestry of vibrant greens and the occasional burst of color from a roadside market. The chatter among us grew more animated as we approached our destination. Zach, ever the planner, was deep into explaining the day's schedule, while the rest of us were busy sharing our expectations and anticipation for Guatape. I couldn't help but notice Robert's unusually upbeat demeanor. Despite the recent hiccup in his personal life, he seemed rejuvenated, clearly looking forward to the trip as a much-needed escape. The bus ride itself felt like a transition from the routine to the realm of adventure, setting the stage for what promised to be an exhilarating exploration.

We were told that Guatape was a beautiful town that draws you in with a subtle, yet penetrating, allure. Guatape is known for a large rock called La Piedra, that has a stair system for tourists to climb. I was stoked to make a Rocky-like Instagram reel for my social media (@Dom.berry.on). I determined that Colombia would be a cool place to grow my social presence.

Zach was beginning to loosen up on the trip. I guess, partly, because he was beginning to see more of the city - and the world was beginning to look larger, owing to his preference for solitude. Zach and I hadn't hung out much coming up to the trip, and we barely knew each other prior, but his open heart and awesome attitude were comforting to me. He was becoming a really good friend, and I enjoyed his company.

The first stop on this day trip tour was a town named El Penol, which was quaint with rustic buildings and churches. Robert and I bought some rings at one of the shops. I also got a cool sombrero.

As we continued our journey, the bus wove through narrow roads lined with verdant hills and blossoming flora. The landscape became increasingly picturesque, with serene lakes peeking through the trees and distant mountains forming a dramatic backdrop. The excitement among us grew palpable as the anticipation of Guatapé's famed charm began to build. We shared stories and jokes, our laughter mixing with the rhythmic hum of the bus engine. Our driver, a lively character with a knack for storytelling journey, kept us entertained with tales of the region's history and folklore. He pointed out landmarks along the way, each story adding a layer of intrigue to the. His enthusiasm was infectious, making the ride feel like a part of the adventure rather than just a commute.

The ride from El Penol to Guatape was exciting. You could see the large looming trees imposing themselves along the paths, and our driver was interesting company. Over the bus speaker system, he stated:

**Driver:** I know you will enjoy the view. One of the best in Colombia!

Guatape enveloped us in its embrace. You could see the rock peaking up above the sky, almost touching the clouds.

Robert started to wake up and chat to two girls next to him who wore leather pants and jackets. They both had sprayed their hair into colors.

Zach and I were beginning to open up to each other. I had always seen him like a reticent child who was only concerned with himself and engrossed in his own affairs. In a sense, I wasn't that keen on getting too familiar with him. I saw him as Robert's friend and accorded him that respect, but in Guatape, Zach began to open up. Partly, since he was beginning to see me from another light.

**Zach:** Luke, sorry about Rob's attitude on the bus earlier.

We were both at the entrance to La Piedra and had to begin the ascent to the top of the rock.

**Luke:** No worries, Zach. I figured that he was just bummed he hasn't landed a solid chick yet, but here, look…

I pointed toward Rob's direction.

**Luke:** He has quite moved on from that.

We both smiled. I had yet to see a smile that broad from him since we began our trip. I was forced to ask him:

**Luke:** So, what do you think of this place?

He studied the surroundings for a moment. I was curious to know what his mind had to say about things. I liked the fact that he was a man of many ideas, even though we had begun our friendship from a distance in previous times.

**Zach:** Well, for a start, the lake system here is next level.

He looked at me in amusement, and I smiled in return. He continued:

**Zach:** But here's what I really think - it's gorgeous, surreal, but it's hot as fuck, and I'm not going to like these stairs.

I joined in with a spirited:

**Luke:** Let's get it, Papi! Step by step, we'll get there soon enough. Let's do it for the view!

In a moment, I saw a truth that was tugging at me for most of my adulthood. The things I blamed my parents for when it came to their divorce were also playing out in all the previous relationships that I had failed to forge into a long-lasting experience. I began to see that, while it's easy to look at our folks' mistakes, it's also necessary to look at our own lives - to watch and see if we were not playing our own part in it all.

As we made our ascent up the large rock, Zach turned to tell me:

**Zach:** I don't think I've seen a city so cool and unique in a long while.

**Luke:** I don't think you go out that often, by the way, Zach.

He chuckled, and I laughed. Robert was brooding.

**Luke:** What's up, Rob? How's the back of the bus treating you?

Rob seemed to be engrossed in a thought. His Tinder account had been reported and deleted. We all figured it could have been the girl whom he had a fallout with who was responsible for it.

**Robert:** Hell hath no fury as a scorned woman.

I tapped his back, and he nodded his head slightly. I knew he was seething, and he had been bruised.

**Luke:** So, guys, Madelein wants to join us for dinner tonight. I was hoping she could come with some friends to lighten up our mood.

Robert made a grimace, then blurted out:

**Robert:** Madelein this. Madelein that! Come on, man! You just got here, and you can't seem to get enough of her name out of your mouth.

I understood his predicament. He was supposed to be the one calling the shots when it came to the women.

**Zach:** Hey man, cool it! Some hours ago, you were in some good company, and now you are acting all grumpy for what?

Zach was one to address issues from a non-biased view, and it was worth it, having him on the team.

I looked toward Robert's direction, and I could see the girls smiling. They were warming up to his charms. Zach and I continued onward and upward. Robert brought the girls to where we were standing and introduced them.

**Robert:** Hey guys, this is Sarah and Francisca.

I studied both girls. Sarah was busty with a gap tooth that was visible when she smiled. I knew where the attraction came from, for Rob, with her. He was a man of big buxom anyways. As for Francisca, she had a lithe body with wide, firm hips. She seemed like the type to work out. From the look in her eyes, I could tell that she was sizing up Zach.

**Robert:** Gentlemen, I've asked these lovely ladies to join us on our boat ride before we head back to Medellin. What do you think?

Classic Robert. Earlier, he was feeling bad at my intention to bring Madelein along on the trip, but here he was planning for some random girls who he met a mere few minutes ago. Seeing that Zach was all for it, I followed suit. We continued up and up until we reached the top - what a view!

The lake system exposed so many luxurious homes right on the waterfront. I turned to Zach and told him:

**Luke:** I want to retire here.

We both chuckled and then tried to find Robert. The descent down, with our two new friends, was easier than the way up. We were excited to eat and then head on for the afternoon boat ride.

The water was a gorgeous green, and the boat ride was exhilarating. The lake was an attraction that drew in thousands of tourists each month. We were able to jump on jet skis and head over to this secret island called La Isla de Labios. It had a rare species of flower along its banks. The flower looked exactly like the lip emoji - I got the perfect photo and posted it to @Dom.Berry.On. The ladies plucked some and decorated their hair with it. Zach was in his research mood again.

**Zach:** This is a rare flower of a certain species that could go extinct.

Francisca had begun to cozy up to him. She was eager to listen, and he was pleased to indulge her.

**Francisca:** There's a soccer match this evening at the Medellin stadium. It's a derby between the two Medellin teams. Would you guys like to go?

The thought of a match excited the boys and we decided that we were going to stake on who would win. The girls chimed in. Sarah and Robert bet against our team, and we staked $20. We still had to get the tickets to the game, so we cut short our boat trip to head towards the stadium.

There's something about South Americans and soccer when you compare it to the United States. Every match feels like a duel between gladiators, fighting to the death. There's a sense of urgency, and there is no small competition. All games seemed like lives depended on them.

There was a massive line of spectators and fans waiting to get tickets for the match, while others made a queue for the teeming crowd to see the game. The uproar from the stadium was deafening. Fans from both sides were singing the names of their players and screaming expletives at each other. Robert and Sarah walked hand-in-hand, followed by Zach and Francisca, while I followed suit behind both couples. I was beginning to miss Madelein.

The five of us sat in the last row of seats. We were lucky enough to get seats, but Francisca was from the town and had influence at the stadium.

There was a beer stand at the stadium, so Zach did the rounds. A pint lingered on each of our hands as we joined the crowd to scream support for the players.

The game was between "Medellin green" and "Medellin red;" they had real names, Atletico Nacional (AN) and Independiente Medellin (DIM), but this was easier for us first-time attendees to follow along. From the announcement box, we could hear the names of the players being called as they filed into the stadium. Robert and Sarah had been in support of Medellin red, while the rest of us rooted for Medellin green.

The referee blew the whistle for the kickoff, and the scramble for victory began. Medellin Red were boosted by the signing of a new Colombian player, so there was a sense that the team would have an edge over Medellin Green. Medellin Green, on the other hand, were the team to beat. They were on top of the league. Of course, these details were made available by Francisca, who was a sportswriter for a local newspaper outlet in Medellin.

Medellin Red registered the first goal within the first two minutes, and Robert and Sarah made their faces towards us, basking in their victory. Zach, Francisca, and I still joined the fans of Medellin Green in raising our voices, regardless. It's one of the beauties of the game - there's always hope until the final whistle. The stadium was filled with people trying to out scream each other.

Going to this game was one of the best decisions ever. Robert and Zach had never been to a game before. I, on the other hand, grew up playing club soccer. I was captain of my high school soccer team and had a special appreciation for the sport. My dad was a die-hard Manchester United fan, so I followed suit. I had been a Premiership fan, which is arguably the best league in the world. The Latin America league wasn't as tough, but man, did they score more goals.

This game was one of the most epic games I had ever seen. It ended up being 4 - 3, Medellin red for the win, and a fight broke out in front of us! The guy starting the fight fell 5 flights off the bleachers. Fucking wild! We snuck out before the game finished, though.

We beat the crowds, leaving the stadium, and went to have dinner. I gave Madelein a ring.

**Madelein:** Hello stranger.

It was refreshing hearing her voice. I wanted to tell her that seeing her had triggered something inside of me. That,during this deafening noise, her voice was more prominent than ever. With a tinge of trepidation, I said:

**Luke:** I was hoping to see you tonight. Do you want to join us for dinner?

I didn't want to seem desperate, but after that night, I had come to realize that - somewhere inside of her - she was willing for me to press on. Although, I wasn't too sure about it.

**Madelein:** Yeah, sounds great. Send me the address.

She hung up. I think she sort of liked the idea of making me chase after her, but I could feel the chemistry building up.

The two girls we were with ended up having other plans, so they didn't leave the game with us. I could feel the tension build up with Robert regarding the ladies. Though the timing worked out okay, Zach chose this moment to gloat, saying:

**Zach:** So, guys, you owe us 20 bucks!

**Robert:** Yeah, you win…

Robert brought out his wallet and placed a $20 bill in Zach's palm. We decided to grab micheladas to alleviate the drama of the ladies, then headed back to our Airbnb.

Madelein called and said that she was coming over to join us. I asked if she could pack some extra stuff if she wanted to come to Cartagena with me. It looked like Zach and Robert might have to find some ladies in Cartagena. I could tell that the lack of lady love was getting to Robert, at least. He called Zach and I to an impromptu meeting:

**Robert:** Guys, I don't think this will work. Why is it necessary to bring ladies along? They are extra baggage, you know.

Zach, being quite a pragmatic fellow, wasn't too aligned with Robert's self-centered approach towards things.

**Zach:** Hey Robert, are we having this conversation because you're not bringing someone?

Zach was staring hard into his face, and I could sense the tension building up. Robert was beginning to warm up for a confrontation.

**Robert:** Dude, what has that got to do with anything? Look at the bills of having to bring extra women along. I am not down with it.

I thought long and hard. How were we to handle this situation? Madelein was already on her way.

**Luke:** But Rob, it's a penthouse. What would we be doing with all that space when we get to Cartagena? Come on dude, stop being a buzzkill.

I left his room with anger and headed towards mine. I called Madelein to ask if she could come with a friend. She said she had some in Cartagena, so I told Robert the good news:

**Luke:** Hey Rob, Madelein has friends in Cartagena. I'm guessing you wouldn't mind now, seeing that you can pair up with one of them, right?

We all laughed. We knew he didn't want to feel left out. His reputation as a ladies' man was beginning to dwindle on this trip, and he wasn't comfortable with that fact.

Madelein invited her friend Sarai. I silently prayed that she would click with Robert, though she seemed a far cry from Rob's expectations. Rob loved women who depended on his attention all the time, but I had a feeling this friend of Madelein's was an independent spirit.

We took a cab to the international airport, while Robert asked Madelein for photos of her friend. The airport staff were struggling to keep up with a barrage of travelers, and we were beginning to get impatient with their services. We were grateful for Madelein, though, as she made it easier for us with her fluency in the local language and ability to communicate with the airport staff. We checked our bags and proceeded toward the terminal.

I had wanted Madelein to sit close to me on the flight, but I had to endure the temporary separation. Soon, I was going to share some time with her, all to myself. I would unfold the yearning in my heart to her.

In Cartagena, we had settled for a penthouse, but the owner told us the arrangements were for three of us and not five, so we were asked to pay more. Robert was nearly losing his head, but Zach and I rallied around the issue so as not to dampen the spirits of the ladies. I paid for Madelein and Sarai. All was well after that.

# The Escapades of Cartagena

## Chapter Five

With the arrangement for the 2 extra guests in the Airbnb resolved, we all began to settle into our respective rooms. It was immediately worked out between Zach and Robert. We had a three-room penthouse with an outdoor jacuzzi and a killer view. Madelein texted Sarai the address, and we planned out the itinerary for our Cartagena experience. We looked towards going to some islands. Daniel had told me about two islands called Pow Pow and Bora Bora. Madelein agreed that these were the places to visit. She had grown up in Cartagena and had some connections for boats.

Robert was still trying to "get his game right" in anticipation for Sarai to show up. He planned out some indoor activities and put on some music while we tried playing card games. Madelein and Zach got along well, and I was stoked to have invited her. When Sarai showed up, we all went downstairs to get her. She was light-skinned and relatively short, with a very pretty face, and I could tell both Robert and Zach were stoked to be in the company of pretty women.

Watching Robert and Sarai was interesting; for one, Robert's ego was being put to test. He always prided himself as the sort of man who could make any lady swoon, but here was Sarai - and she was not one to fall for his charms. Through Madelein, I came to realize that Sarai was recently coming out of a heartbreak. Her relationship of five years had ended, so the only reason she agreed to join their trip was to unwind. I felt a kinship with her since I had just recovered from my heartbreak. I knew what she felt, in a way, so I decided that I was going to speak with Robert about it later. For now, we needed to plan our trip to the islands.

As the day progressed, I noticed subtle changes in Sarai's demeanor. Initially, she seemed reserved and distant, but as she engaged more with the group, a flicker of her old self began to emerge. During a brief pause in the conversation, I saw her sharing a genuine laugh with Madelein and the others. It was clear that the trip was starting to lift her spirits, and there was something reassuring about seeing her gradually open up. This small shift was a reminder of the healing power of new experiences and good company. Sarai's presence, although quiet, was becoming an integral part of our group dynamic, and I hoped that with time, she would find the solace and distraction she needed.

Madelein, having experience with tourism, made some calls and planned the trip herself. She was able to secure a boat for Colombian prices, as opposed to the inflated "gringo prices" we would have been charged if we went alone. I was beginning to see Madelein from different angles; not only was she gorgeous, but she was also smart, resourceful, and ever-willing to help out sort issues.

On our second night in Cartagena, we all went to a discotheque. Madelein and I got some alone time together since she was having cramps and wasn't in the mood to go out. Sarai was in high spirits that evening, so Madelein was able to snap out of her mood and rally!

That night, we really got the chance to talk. I told her of my roots in Venice and a few of my escapades with past relationships. We even joked about my long hair, which I wore as a child, that made me look like a girl - and the name Meghan etched on the concrete patch in front of the house because my parents thought I was going to be a girl and didn't reveal my gender during my Mom's pregnancy. I was content with the fact that I could make her laugh. It was obvious she was enjoying my company.

**Luke:** What about you, Madelein? What's your story?

**Madelein:** Do you really want to know?

She looked at me with a piercing gaze. I was sitting at our table with a bottle of champagne. Robert and Zach took shots with Sarai and were dancing with some of the nearby women. I was sipping on my drink, patiently waiting for Madelein to speak. I fixed my gaze on her, too. If it took forever, I was going to listen to anything she had to tell me. I was feeling great.

**Madelein:** For starters, my folks are from Medellin, but I grew up in Cartagena for a while, in a town not too far away from here. Mom married my dad quite young, and she had me when she was young.

She paused to show me a picture of her mom, Sandra, on her phone. It was easy to see where Madelein got her looks from.

**Madelein:** Pretty, isn't she?

I nodded in agreement. As I listened to her speak, I wanted her to keep talking till the end of time. There was no place I wanted to be other than to be right beside her. There was nothing I desired more than that moment. She spoke of her aunt, Paola, who lived in Cartagena for most of her life. She called to tell her she was in town and asked if I was willing to see her aunt. In a way, I felt uncertain. I was just getting to know her, and I did not want to seem like I was coming on too hard. Besides, I wanted to take things slow and felt like meeting her people was like laying claim to an intention for going further.

The next day, she was brighter. True to her word, the cramps had given her some relief, and we all got set for the trip to the islands. The islands were in a world of their own. The waters glistened, and the inhabitants were boisterous. Tents and parties littered the place, and it was difficult to tell visitors from residents, but there was something about the ambiance that held sway over our consciousness. In the spirit of the islands, the five of us let ourselves roam free.

We were all vibing. Robert and Sarai seemed inseparable, and it felt like they were reading the others' minds when you watched them. Zach was chilling, enjoying the mood. We were on the water with good drinks and great company. I made a mental note to get with Zach later and see how he was feeling.

On the islands, there were beaches of all sorts - small and large. We drank from the exotic coconut fruits offered by the vendors. You could see boats traveling to different places from a distance. It was an interesting scene.

Paola put in a good word to one of the island bars, and we took the boat to Bora Bora first. Interesting place to see - super preppy, painted in all white. Great cabanas and awesome music. Madelein wanted me to take a bunch of photos of her. From the way she asked me questions about what I did and what my plans were, it was obvious that she seemed to take interest.

Madelein told me of how her aunt and grandma, Claudia, had been strong pillars for her after leaving her mom's house at a young age. It was an inspiring story, and it made me respect her much more as a person.

Although she was a young and beautiful 18-year-old, it was clear she had already experienced so much in life for someone so young. It was inspirational, really - I felt privileged for living the life I did, with the opportunities that I had been given.

We went to an outdoor aquarium next. Madelein told us we could swim with dolphins here. I had done the experience during a past trip to Cancun, but would do it again, especially with her. Seeing her smile and express so much happiness made me never want to leave. Zach and Robert recorded Madelein, Sarai, and me swimming with the dolphins. After the excursion, we all exited the dolphin enclosure and quickly ate some of the available snacks. A few minutes later, Sarai broke the ice:

**Sarai:** So, tell me, Luke. What's your deal with Madelein?

The question caught me by surprise, in a way. I had never thought for a second that Madelein gave her friend *any* hints that something more was attached to our closeness. I wasn't clear on the direction of our relationship, but I should answer carefully.

On one hand, I was yet to express my desire for something more to Madelein. On the other hand, I didn't know exactly how to qualify the relationship. How was I so sure that Madeleine was thinking in the same direction? Of course, I desired her company, but desire can be a delicate thing. It can be birthed on a shaky foundation. What if my desire was misplaced and merely a function of attraction? What if I wasn't certain of my own feelings? Lots of "buts" and "maybes" filled my heart, but I was as honest as possible with Sarai.

**Luke:** I really can't tell.

Sarai was about to cut a chunk from a fish in her soup, but she dropped the spoon at my statement and stared straight into my eyes.

**Sarai:** Amigo, you can't tell what? Do you think every young man Madelein meets gets to meet me?

This time, I could see Madelein in tapping Sarai's legs with her feet. She avoided my face and stared right into the soup. I found it sweet, in a sense, but I also felt sorry for her. I know the last thing she wanted was to be made to seem like she was desperate for something deep and tangible with me.

**Luke:** What I mean is that Madelein and I haven't really gotten around to discussing much about this relationship. We are still getting to know bits and pieces of ourselves.

Sarai eyeballed me from side to side and laughed. I was at a loss for her attitude. Why was she laughing? I could not understand the point of it. What was funny? Here I was, sweating all over. I was concerned about my words and how they might affect my chances with Madelein, but here was Sarai, laughing at my predicament. I felt a flush on my face but tried to stay as composed as possible.

**Sarai:** Amigo, it's not that serious; I was just teasing you. I'm sure you two would get along quite well. I see the way you look at her. She is beautiful, isn't she?

This time, she was looking at Madelein. Madelein managed to find her voice.

**Madelein:** Sarai, stop bothering him, loca.

She managed to give me a "sorry" look this time around and made a sign of feeling for me. I winked at her and mouthed silently that I understood her. I could sense that Sarai was aware of our nonverbal cues, but she concentrated on her fish soup.

After eating, Sarai told us she had one more stop and insisted on taking us along. What I wasn't expecting was that she would drive us to her home. I am not certain if Madelein knew about it, but the experience was quite interesting.

Sarai was young as well - 18 and very pretty. She was from Medellin but was living in Cartagena because it's the place to be. I wondered what Robert and Zach thought of her. We saw some of Sarai's friends at the bar, Angelo and Miguel, both tall. Miguel was full of questions, seeing I was from the States.

**Miguel:** Do you know LeBron James? Oh, he is my favorite. How about Steph Curry?

I could barely give an answer before being barraged by another set of questions. We spoke about the NBA games. He was a fan of the Los Angeles Lakers. As for Angelo, he had a reticent demeanor. Sarai and Madelein had gone to take photos, and I was left alone with the boys. I tried to ask Angelo what his favorite sport was, and he said flat out said:

**Angelo:** Fútbol, obvio!

Soon after, we all cruised back to the Airbnb to continue the party.

Miguel dragged me into my room and proceeded to show me pictures of his favorite players. Pictures of LeBron James, Michael Jordan, and Dwyane Wade overwhelmed me. He challenged me to a one-on-one game at the gym, but I just wanted to party.

**Miguel:** Madelein, what do you think?

She smiled.

**Madelein:** Miguel, loco, let me talk with Luke.

Madelein and I walked to the jacuzzi in the penthouse, when we were joined later by Robert, who said:

**Robert:** Sarai's friends left to go get us a table.

We got ready and joined the others at Club Z. When we were out, the world felt smaller, as Madelein and I lost ourselves to the music. Sarai popped something in Robert's mouth and hinted that if he wanted to feel the moment, he should tone it down with the drinks. We had a couple of bottles of Don Julio at the table, and the liquor started to flow; I wasn't a stranger to euphoria and was getting in my zone. At the frat house back in college, I got down. We got booted off campus for hazing and partying too much.

With Madelein, however, the euphoria was a different experience. She was getting groovy in the moment as we swayed side-to-side to the beat and wrapped our hands around ourselves. Hers on my shoulders and mine around her waist. In those minutes, the world around us was nonexistent. We were simply in a world of our own - a planet away from everyone else. I whispered into her ears:

**Luke:** Can I kiss you?

She rested her chin on my shoulders and whispered back.

**Madelein:** Did you have to ask Luke?

I liked the way she called my name. There was something inviting in it, like she had known me longer than the few days we had spent together. I turned my face to hers. My heart was skipping like it was running out of the ribcage. As our lips locked, I could feel her breath rising. Our teeth jammed, and we both laughed. Robert came over and tapped my shoulders.

**Robert:** Hey dude, can I have a word with you?

I kissed Madelein on the side of her cheek and told her I was coming back.

**Luke:** What's up, Rob?

Robert looked upset, and I could notice the sweat dripping down his neck.

**Robert:** This chick is shutting me out, man. She keeps giving me mixed signals. One moment, she is here, and the next, she wants to be all by herself.

**Luke:** Relax, man. Babe is going through the motions; she just got over a heartbreak.

I was hoping with that revelation he would reason with me, but it only made him more adamant.

**Robert:** That's crap, man. She should have just stayed behind.

**Luke:** Robert, it is not always about you, man. Take a chill pill.

I tried to hold his hands, but he shoved my hands aside and walked out of the club. I saw Zach walking up to him. They walked out of the club; then both walked back in. Madelein and Sarai were seated together now, so when Robert and Zach walked up to the bar, I joined them. Robert seemed to be calmer now, but we sat side-by-side, with him in our middle.

**Robert:** Guys, maybe we shouldn't have come. We've been spending so much, and it just feels like there's nothing special about it all.

I stayed quiet since I did not know what to make of Robert's attitude. I felt maybe Zach was in a better position to speak with him, since he was the one who encouraged him to come back into the club. So, I signaled for him to say something.

**Zach:** Hey dude, I know you need company. It isn't "like we have spent so much for nothing" since we came here. You should not take Sarai's rejection to heart. Besides, you told me Luke spoke of her dealing with a heartbreak.

Madelein was walking up to us, so I rose up to meet her. I held her hand as we walked to a corner of the club.

**Madelein:** Sarai wants to go back to Medellin. I have been trying to speak to her and to stay back, but she feels like Robert is coming on too strong. Since she isn't tied down now, she feels pressured to pair up with him.

**Luke:** I will speak with her myself then.

**Madelein:** Thank you.

She squeezed my hands in hers. The night felt good, and my buzz felt great. It was 2:30 am. I walked up to Sarai and told her to take a walk with me. Robert and Zach were still at the bar, but this time, I could see a more cheerful Robert with empty bottles between him and Zach.

**Luke:** Sarai, I am sorry for how you feel. I know there has been tension between you and Robert. Here's the deal: you do *not* have to feel any pressure whatsoever, and you should feel free to express yourself around us. We are glad to have you around and appreciate your company.

**Sarai:** Thank you, Luke.

She gave me a slight hug.

**Sarai:** And thanks for making Madelein feel safe, too.

We both walked a bit away from the club to a side of the street facing the club, and I could see two figures hidden with their backs leaning on a building, making out. We walked back into the club, and Sarai joined the ladies while I went to my buddies. In high spirits, Robert said:

**Robert:** Luke, man, I've got a solution to this! I am going to take one of these lassies around to your room, and you'll have to find a place in the living room to spend the rest of the night.

**Luke:** Deal Robert. Anything to make you happy.

Zach gave a squint, and I returned it. Sacrifices had to be made to placate Robert's ego - it was better that way for the sanity of everyone.

The next day was a repeat. We took a boat to the island bar Pow Pow, but Robert was complaining so much about money that it became annoying. Sarai turned to Zach, who was keeping better company. Robert didn't take to this well, which made the vibe worse. I was just happy to be with Madelein here. Pow Pow was awesome and had a bunch of golden statues and crazy white pools with the bluest of waters. I was in Heaven!

We created excuses to carve out time for ourselves on the island. Our major challenge was getting Robert and Sarai to have a connection. She was still hurting, and oftentimes, she found Madelein and me to interrupt - as we tired shared moments together talking. We knew it was because she wasn't enjoying Robert's company, but there was something interesting about her, and she seemed to like Zach's personality more and more.

After talking with Madelein, we jumped into the main pool, and an infamous game of "Truth or Dare?" started. Robert organized the game and started writing examples of "dares" people could opt for on the Notes app on his phone.

When it was Sarai's turn, her dare on Robert's phone read: "Pick a person out, kiss them for 15 minutes, and tell us what they taste like." At this, Robert got excited since he thought she would choose him, but to his surprise, she picked Zach, who had to bail himself out by emptying the cocktail of drinks mixed in a cup - consequently for not carrying out the dare.

After hours in the sun, we took the boat back to the dock by our penthouse. Madelein and I went to park in the town center. The park was large, sprawling with enormous trees of different species. It was a colorful place. She showed me all the different birds of paradise on the trees that came down sometimes to look at tourists - which is where I first spoke my heart out to her.

After that kiss at the club that night, she continued opening up to me. There was this unwritten code that we were an item, although we were yet to define it. We sat on a bench, holding hands and watching the wonders of the different species of birds and their beautiful colors.

**Luke:** Madelein, I've been trying to refrain from speaking empty words to you. I've been trying to guard my heart from bursting open with excitement. I've been trying to be careful not to say the things I do not mean to you. To be honest, when we first met, I had never imagined we would have been this close. After that first night at the Discotheque 818, I had imagined I made a fool of myself and lost you.

This time, I was holding both of her hands and staring right into her face. There was a faint smile on her lips and a curiosity in her eyes. She was the most beautiful woman I had ever seen, and I knew crossing the seas to be in Colombia with her was totally worth it. I continued:

51

**Luke:** Madelein, trust me when I say that I want to get to know you more than you could ever imagine. I want you to be my woman. Not just some girl I have come to meet on a trip, but one that I could see myself with for a lifetime.

At this, she laughed, and I could see her face flushing with embarrassment. Some kids were running around in the park with sticks, mimicking a sword duel, and I could see that she was worried so they would not poke their eyes with the sticks.

**Madelein:** Take it easy, guys, be careful with that.

I felt open and vulnerable. It had been a long while since I bared my heart out to a woman, and I never imagined that I was going to find love in Colombia. Let alone on Instagram, and here I was, in the presence of a woman who would turn my world upside down.

**Madelein:** Luke, when I met you, I was struggling with my life. My heart can bruise easily, and I don't know what your plans are. Maybe you feel this way now because I've been consistent with you these past few days. Maybe you don't really know all of me just yet. Maybe you don't know if you will feel this same way about me in the coming days. Or months. Maybe you would go back to the States to some chick you have been dating, and you will begin where you left off. I don't know, Luke. I like the idea of starting something with you. You are a good man. You make me feel safe. You listen, and you are there for me. But I don't know if this is just your nature playing out as a term of endearment.

She squeezed my hands. Her eyes were pleading to be reassured.

**Luke:** Madelein, the truth is, I'm falling for you. I am not just saying this because of these few days. Neither am I just saying empty words. I am opening up my feelings because, for a long while, I have yet to meet a woman who stirred up the hidden parts of me. I know for both of us the future seems unsure. I know it may be like we are just aiming at nothing because we barely know each other. But this much I know - you are one woman in whom I have come to find pleasure.

**Madelein:** But Luke, pleasure is not enough. I have goals to meet. I have desires that I crave for. I have ambitions to be met. I can't just leave all of this behind.

I knew that she was touching a deep part of the conversation. What would happen if we both decided to move the relationship forward? Would she have to leave Colombia to join me in the States? What were her ambitions, and how could I fit into them? There was something about her that was determined and feisty, which showed in her influence with others. I recalled that party at the cruise liner - how she moved about everywhere, and every member of the organizing team seemed to run around at her command. It was true. How did I expect her to leave all this behind? Her work and efforts? How did I expect her to leave all that to travel across the seas to be with me? Although we were yet to talk about any of it, I knew that "talk" would come up.

# Falling In Love

## Chapter Six

Madelein turned out to be a breath of fresh air. I thought that, with women, I knew what I wanted, but meeting Madelein made it obvious I had been missing out on so much more - a rare gem. She had a finesse to her gait, a thoughtfulness to her words, and an aura of peace radiated around her that made me feel like nothing in the world could go wrong with her by my side.

That conversation with Madelein at the park in Cartagena opened my mind up to parts of me that I had yet to realize resided in me. I knew I was the sort of guy who never remained with one girl for a long time. When it comes to women, I have always been a rolling stone. For me, being with them was more of an adventure than commitment. It was difficult to commit myself to them in the long term, partly because of the heartbreaks I had encountered - and mostly because my parents' break-up had left a void in my heart.

For some reason, I missed my sister, Cayley. I decided to give her a call.

**Luke:** I think I have found the one.

She stayed quiet for a moment. In the background, I could hear some sound, and I strained my ears to try and make out what the sounds were.

**Cayley:** Luke, you know this is like the umpteenth time I've heard you tell me about meeting "the one." What's so different this time?

She was right. I had always started off with this much excitement when meeting a new girl or entering a new relationship. In the past, with some, it seemed like I was going to remain with them, but after a couple of months - or, at most, in a short span of years - we parted ways.

I had to think of some valid reason for my claim this time. Her question was more of a wake-up call for me to validate my claims. Did I really love Madelein? Was I using her as a rebound? How was I certain about knowing what I wanted with her?

**Luke:** Listen, Sis, it's sweet of you to prove my feelings this way, but the deal is, I think I might love her and want a future with her.

I could hear the shuffling of her feet. She seemed to be busy with something at the other end, hence the noise.

**Cayley:** Luke, I care for your well-being, and I want the best for you. Don't take my question the wrong way. I want you to be happy, and I hope you find what you seek with her. I gotta go, love you.

It was our last night in Cartagena, and Zach suggested we step out to a club, but Robert suggested we have a jacuzzi party at the penthouse. As for me, I didn't care. I was still in my head about the conversation I had with Madelein at the park. Madelein rested her head on my chest, and all I could think of was to run my hands through her hair. We ended up having a jacuzzi party and buying more bottles of Don Julio.

The next day, we woke up with a hangover. My head was splitting up, but Madelein had wokenup earlier to get us all some coffee. We gathered our baggage and left for Medellin. Luckily, it was a quick flight, and we were happy to arrive back in Medellin.

**Zach:** Cartagena was fun right?

**Everyone:** Hell yeah!

Robert was gulping down a bottle of beer and seemed uninterested in the conversation.

**Robert:** Dude, Cartegena was just there; nothing special about it, man.

I knew it was because he wasn't getting the attention he had hoped he would get from Sarai.

**Luke:** Dude, why are you acting up? Is this all because of Sarai?

I sat down close to him on the couch. I wanted to get a beer for us both, but I decided on water instead. There was something about Madelein that made me want to be a better man, and I decided that if she were going to take me seriously, I needed to quiet my excesses on vacation and make her see my genuineness.

**Robert:** No, Luke, we spent quite a lot of funds on this trip, and I wasn't expecting it to be this expensive.

I knew he was exaggerating things. After all, this was one hell of a trip. If we were in the States, we would not have had the sort of privilege that we had over here - the Airbnb was cheaper, and we had the company of beautiful women.

**Luke:** Robert, I just think you feel that way because Sarai didn't give you any.

Sarai had given Zach a long hug the day she departed. Robert didn't get what Zach got.

**Robert:** She was just all over Zach like I didn't exist. Man, if you don't mind, let's forget about the Cartagena business and think of something else. Besides, I want to take a nap.

Robert went to his room to sleep, and I left the apartment to take a stroll. Medellin was beautiful. The city smelled of flowers, and the sky let loose some rainfall. I stood under a patio cover to wait for the rain to die down. I wanted to remain in Medellin, to have my roots deeply planted. I desired to be with Madelein. At this moment, nothing else mattered; I just wanted to be with her. That evening, Madelein called and said she wanted us to get dinner at one of her favorite restaurants.

She wore a purple dress and beautiful makeup. She carried a purple bag, and she wore purple shoes. I, on the other hand, wore a turtleneck shirt, black jeans, and the sombrero I bought in Guatape. She was waiting for me when I got there, and I could tell that she had paid extra attention to her looks.

**Luke:** You are beautiful,Madelein! Where have you been all my life?

She laughed that laughter that always made me feel at ease. She was not just beautiful but also soothing to my soul. We made our orders, and I asked for a glass of champagne.

**Luke:** You know, they say the stars are captured in every champagne bottle. What do you think?

She was wrestling with a beef steak, but her hands were steady, and I watched her precision. Even to the most mundane of things, she was a woman with poise.

**Madelein:** If that be the case, then let us drown ourselves in the clouds.

We both laughed, and then a guy walked up to our table:

**Guy**: Excuse me, sir, that lady over there asked me to send you a wine.

I looked at my side, and guess who I saw? It was a girlfriend from college. She was in the company of some ladies, and I must confess, she looked so hot that I was tempted to stand up to go say hi - but I could see Madelein's face, all scrunched up and perturbed that evening was beginning to take a different shape.

**Luke:** Tell her thanks; much appreciated.

I nodded to the waiter and was uneasy about facingMadelein. I knew she felt slighted, and I didn't know what she was thinking. I did not want to defend myself so as not to look like I had something to hide. She asked first:

**Madelein:** Who is she?

A part of me was so excited that I could feel a sense of jealousy, as it meant she was beginning to take me more seriously. I liked it.

**Luke:** She's a girl I dated back when I was your age. I'm surprised that, of all places, I would see her here, in Medellin.

She looked at me with a piercing gaze, the kind that was prying into me to see if I was lying.

**Luke:** Hey Madelein, I wouldn't be feeling this way with you if I had some skeletons in my closet, you know.

She signaled to the waiter.

**Madelein:** How much is our bill?

I held her hands as she grabbed her purse and took care of the bill.

**Madelein:** Luke, I want to go home.

She was not happy. I was bothered.

**Luke:** Just listen to me, Madelein, and believe me. It was just a friendly gesture, and I haven't seen that girl in years. I didn't know she even remembered my face.

I held her waist as she walked fast out of the restaurant, hailing a taxi. I waved the taxi off.

**Luke:** Listen, babe.If there's anyone that matters, it's you.

I motioned to kiss her forehead. She stayed calm, and I drew her close to me, and we hugged. I kissed her forehead again, and this time, she drew closer with her lips to mine and locked my lips in hers. I felt it again, the flutters in my tummy. I could not remember feeling this way for anyone.

As I lay there, restless and staring at the ceiling, the weight of the situation grew heavier. The intimacy we shared had brought a whirlwind of emotions, and I was caught in the storm of what-ifs and maybes. I could see our time together as a fleeting moment of joy, but the reality of our impending separation loomed large. The connection we had felt so deep, yet the uncertainty of how to nurture it across continents was daunting. My thoughts raced through memories of our shared laughter and tender moments, contrasting sharply with the inevitable distance that would soon separate us. I wondered if our bond could survive the physical separation, or if it was destined to be a beautiful chapter in the story of our lives, left behind as we moved forward.

That night, I could not sleep. I rolled on my king-sized mattress and thought long and hard about what I wanted to do next, seeing that I was going to be leaving soon for the States. A decision had to be reached. It was time to decide, once and for all, how to approach my relationship with her. I awoke something in her, even though she was trying hard to fight it.

I could tell she was still undecided, but her feelings were beginning to betray her. She was catching the love bug, but I had to decide fast. What was I to do when I got back to the States? Our flight was scheduled for the 12th of September. We arrived in Medellin on the 2nd of September. I didn't know what to make of the future for us, but I knew that I was certain I wanted to be with her.

We flew back on the 12th of September, and I called my realtor on the 13th with instructions to list my house for sale. Colombia was calling out to me, or should I say, Madelein was calling out to me. We spoke every day, and I could barely wait to go back.

I asked myself if I was sure I was doing the right thing. I was in love but scared. What if I sold my house and moved to Colombia and found that Madelein didn't want me as badly as I thought she did? I wanted to tell her about my decision to sell my house. I held up on it until I was sure.

My uncle died the week I got back, which left me down in the dumps. I took some time off work - they gave me three days of bereavement. I needed more time and was told to take my remaining vacation. One day, on my time off from work, I spoke to my sister about next steps. She made me some toast and poured hot English breakfast tea into a white teacup for me.

**Cayley:** I miss you, Luke. How is Madelein?

It felt like she read my mind. I took a bite of the bread and a sip of the British breakfast tea she made herself. I was stalling on purpose since she had the tendency to see through things without emotions. I needed that.

**Luke:** Cayley, I am thinking of moving to Colombia to settle down.

She took a seat and sat close to me as she placed her tea on the table.

**Cayley:** Luke, have you taken the time to think about your career? All that you would be leaving behind? You make so much money right now. Are you sure you want to do this? Luke, you are my brother, and I always want you to feel safe and rest assured in whatever decision you take.

She looked at me blankly and waited for me to speak.

**Luke:** You know me, all my life, I have been trying hard to fit into an idea. I have worked hard to build a life that isn't really mine. This time, I want something different. I feel it deep in my bones. I guess I needed that trip to nudge me back to reality.

Cayley gave a sigh. She could tell I had made up my mind on what I wanted, and there was no going back now.

**Cayley:** Well, Luke, you know you can always come back home whenever you feel like things are not going as planned.

That night, as I had trouble sleeping, I thought of what my motivation had been living all the while. I had been living for my parents' reputation. As a son of immigrants, I had, in a sense, achieved the American Dream. I had a well-paying job, and I bought a house. My folks were proud of me, but I had never really lived for myself. It seemed like I was in the rat race just to prove a point. To what end was I chasing a career if it was at the expense of my happiness? I had been living all my life just to work.

From when I could walk and talk, the idea of "what the future would be like?" was laid out by my folks. In the community of immigrants, they had a way of comparing each other's children. Many immigrants worked their asses off just to place their children in good schools, so they could earn good grades and get high-paying jobs. It was a huge disappointment to any family whose children did not meet up with the expectations.

There was a story of a family who had labored to send their only son, Thomas, to Harvard University. His parents were both Mexicans and related to my Mom's side of the family. Thomas spent one semester at Harvard and decided that he was going to become a rockstar. His parents were ashamed as the news spread through the circle of friends that they kept.

As for Thomas, he dropped out of Harvard and didn't live up to anything. His parents never forgave him for it. It was a common story told to the children of immigrant parents in our family.

Growing up in the shadow of such high expectations can be both a burden and a motivator. The pressure to excel is a constant companion, driving us to achieve more than what might be expected of the average person. For many of us, the stakes are not just personal but familial. Every accomplishment or failure feels magnified, as if our actions are a direct reflection of our parents' sacrifices. The drive to succeed is fueled by a deep-seated desire to honor their struggles and to carve out a place where their dreams, once placed in us, can finally flourish. It's this dual sense of responsibility—to live up to personal goals while also validating our parents' hard work—that shapes our aspirations and choices.

Yet, amid the relentless pursuit of success, it's easy to lose sight of our own desires and well-being. We often find ourselves caught between the need to meet external expectations and the need to forge our own path. The high standards we set for ourselves can sometimes overshadow our personal happiness and fulfillment. As we strive to surpass the achievements of our parents, it's crucial to remember that our journey is also about finding our own sense of purpose and contentment. Balancing these expectations with self-compassion becomes essential, allowing us to honor our heritage while also creating a life that is uniquely ours.

To be a child of an immigrant is to have high standards for yourself. It is a life of impression. We have to show our parents that their efforts are not in vain. We need to prove to our extended relatives that we are doing better off than we would in foreign lands and prove to ourselves also that we could live better lives than those of our folks.

I thought hard about the dreams I had nurtured as a child while playing sports. I recall one game I went to with my school team, and after I didn't "start" on the first squad, my mother went deep into conversation about how I was wasting their efforts to engage in meaningless sports.

**Mom:** How many people do you think make it out there in sports? One injury, and it's all over. Luke, you had better be serious with your studies. With good grades, you can rest assured that you are going to get settled and get a good job.

My dad wasn't impressed, either, at my sporting prowess at the time. For him, it was mere youthful exuberance. What they wanted from me was that I became a complete American who had a career to chase after. Well, I made that happen, and now I wasn't feeling it anymore. I had lived my life for them and, in the process, convinced myself that this was what I wanted.

I decided then and there that I was going to carve a new path. I was going to kick ass in sports, which I did, but also have a different plan A. Financial freedom was the goal. Working for someone else's dream was depriving myself of my own dreams. What if I could earn enough so that I could go wherever I wanted and do whatever I wanted to do? What if I built my own empire and made myself a brand to be reckoned with? I didn't want to be confined to a space and be controlled by someone else.

Those few days in Colombia and the aftereffects made me realize that freedom was a gift anyone could offer to himself and, to be truly free and successful, meant to be in a position where I could control things at my whim. This was a new dream. That night, while lying in bed, it dawned on me that I was meant to find Madeleinto find myself. I just had to build up the courage to make the dream a reality.

I called Madelein the next day and shared my thoughts with her.

**Madelein:** Luke, are you certain about this? I don't want you feeling like you have to rush into anything right now. Please take your time to think about it.

It was natural for her to feel that way, but it did not matter what she felt. My heart was set on my freedom. Every decision was bringing me closer to Madelein, and this newfound zeal was driven by a hunger that surpassed whatever challenges the future had in store for me.

# Life Changing Decisions

## Chapter Seven

B elieve it or not, some things in life hurt more than being hit on the balls. On a scale of 1-10, it's fair to say being hit on the balls counts as 9. It's said that nothing compares to the pain of childbirth, which is probably a 10, but there are certain events that just plain hurt. One of them was losing my uncle.

Uncle Guedo wasn't just a relative; he was a mentor and a friend. His charisma was magnetic, drawing people in with his effortless charm and genuine warmth. He had a way of making every moment special, whether it was through his infectious laughter or the stories he'd tell that always seemed to have a touch of adventure. He was the kind of person who could turn an ordinary day into an unforgettable experience. I remember the countless weekends spent in his company, where he taught me to ride my first bike with a patient hand and a playful spirit. Those driving lessons were more than just lessons; they were lessons in life, filled with laughter, encouragement, and the kind of wisdom that only someone who genuinely cared could impart.

Uncle Guedo was the first person to buy me a bicycle. The first to take me to driving lessons. After my parents separated, I grew a bond with him. I looked up to this guy. He was a slick Italian dude who was so suave, all the time.

He took me out to sporting events and the cinema. He was the kind of person who never imposed himself on you but allowed you to flow with him at your own pace. He was patient as I learned from my mistakes.

I recall a fishing trip the family went on. We rode on a boat named Lucy. We took sandwiches and freshly squeezed juice from his farm. We had a family friend with small farm and a ranch, and one perk of being around the farm was that you could always get fresh juice or milk. I recall those days like they were yesterday.

We caught a huge Marlin fish on this trip and when we got back, I couldn't contain my excitement. This was my first time seeing a fish be caught alive, besides what I watched on TV. It was a pleasantly memorable experience.

Uncle Guedo previously had a falling out with my aunt but showed me how relationships could be civil and I appreciated that. With how much he impacted my life, I needed time off work to recover. I even sought help from the therapist, who I saw after my previous relationship.

I had to make some arrangements. I was placed on three days of bereavement, followed by vacation and then a leave of absence. Seeing my therapist for weekly counseling sessions was a blessing. I had imagined seeing a therapist would make the pain go away quicker, but talking about it for just one hour of the day was not nearly enough to ease the pain of a lifetime of memories. I needed more than therapy.

I needed a break from work and everything I was engaged with. Work had become a drudgery and, truth be told, after finding out my uncle died, a part of me sunk into a void. I couldn't imagine my Uncle Guedo was gone. He was barely 50 years old, and in my mind, he was going to live for a long time. It had been three years since I last saw him and the last time we spoke on the phone, I promised to visit him. In a sense, I felt laden with guilt. I blamed myself for many things - the times I did not call to check on him, and the times I promised to visit and didn't...

My uncle's death created a sense of urgency in me. What use was living to accrue so much, when someday I was going to die? Although I mourned Uncle Guedo, the truth is, he inspired me to live a robust life like he did.

I had been getting bids for my place in San Diego. One was from a young couple who had just had a baby girl and were interested in getting the apartment since the man had gotten a promotion at work and wanted to continue moving up the social ladder. There were also members from my fraternity who were interested - and willing to pay tens of thousands of dollars more for it.

I partially felt a sense of loyalty to my frat brothers; but in the spirit of Uncle Guedo, my new lens on life gave me a particular perspective I couldn't ignore - as a man, and as a couple, this apartment was a motivation, a "why." I told both parties to give me some days to think about it.

I sold my house for just under $1 million and was stoked. I was able to use this money to help make investments that would shape the rest of my life, or so I thought.

After having sold my San Diego house, I was living in Venice at my mom's house for some time, while traveling back and forth to Colombia to see Madelein. She was glad to see me, while I needed to reflect on how to invest the funds I earned from the sale of the house; and I knew that I had to decide fast.

I outlined the areas I felt were possible and worth investing in. After brainstorming with Zach, we settled on three areas that I noted in my notepad - gold or jewelry, traveling, and property investment. Gold was an area I had interest in, due to my background and expertise in mining commodities; and it was always in demand, so it was worth immense value. Since Madelein was experienced with tourism in Medellin and felt that might be a lucrative business, I felt the travel industry could be worth tapping into, as she could offer ideas, tips, and advice. Finally, property investment. Selling my house for a higher amount than I purchased meant I was motivated to acquire more properties to continue growing those earnings.

Zach and I had some interesting moments, but he was way better than the last time I saw him. He went back to school to finish his education and it was wonderful seeing him put behind the hurt of the past. I asked him if he was ready for a relationship.

**Zach:** Come on Luke, I think that is beyond me right now.

I understood his plight. Love could be hard and arduous when thinking about it. It takes fortitude to let go of yourself, knowing quite well that you might end up with your heart shattered to smithereens; but when you are faced with it, it is always a risk worth taking. Love requires some form of humility and having to express parts of ourselves that we held dear, so we could - ultimately - be one with someone else.

I continued with my plans to move to Colombia. I looked into some Airbnb apartments, but I needed to get Madelein's consent also. I wasn't flying solo this time, I had Madelein to consider.

The week before leaving for Colombia, Zach and I went out for some drinks, and it was wild. Zach had grown a reputation for being a ladies' man. He introduced me to some women who I eventually had to ward off; but, for the first time, I was also worried for Zach.

Normally, I am comfortable finding my friends and myself amid random women; but having met Madelein, things had become different. I could tell that Zach was on a rebound, so we spoke with Robert on a video call. It was exciting seeing him again too. He had grown his hair longer.

The trip back to Colombia was different this time. There was a precision to it. I was trying to see how I could forge a new identity different from what I knew. I settled for a penthouse in Provenza.

I chose Provenza for the hype. It is a lovely place with lots of flowers and trees, a dream location for tourists. Since I was coming solo, I told Madelein to move in with me at the penthouse. She was stoked! She asked about getting an Albino Pomeranian dog; I couldn't tell her no, especially with her so happy about the potential to live with the new dog.

Truth is, I was excited that we had all the time to ourselves this time - so Madelein picked out the new dog, who is now known as Angel. She has blue eyes and a pink nose.

At night, Provenza comes alive with a beehive of activities. You can hear music from speakers, and you can easily forget where you are. It's hard to tell if one is in Colombia when the DJ begins to play a wide range of songs from reggae to hip-hop.

Madelein was a fan of reggaeton music and whenever she sang along to the songs, I couldn't help but be enamored by her fluidity.

Being closer to her meant getting to know each other. For one, I began to see that she was a woman with a focus - not one to be easily swayed by mere ideas.

She wanted to know what my intentions for work would be, once I arrived in Colombia, seeing as I was planning to leave my current job. I wanted to let loose; I chose Provenza for that purpose. In Provenza, feelings of timelessness were so profound, with how much excitement existed to get lost in.

I liked the idea of managing property and renting it out, as it seemed like something I could have control over. I was taking my investments more seriously and needed to find strategies for new opportunities. I was confident that investing and managing property would make sense, with Provenza becoming a hotter tourist destination.

Madelein and I looked at destinations that would attract value. She was quite resourceful and one of the perks of having her around was that I had someone to brainstorm with.

It felt nice having her presence around each morning when, waking up. Our love felt tangible, even though we had yet to say those magic words to each other. Being around her gave me more determination in life.

The Provenza penthouse was owned by an American, named Chris. There was always a mad rush for accommodation, with so many people wanting to be there - which meant a strong need for apartments or other lodging.

I wanted to convince Chris to sell the penthouse to me, but he made it clear - that regardless of whatever price I offered - he wasn't going to let go of it. He gave me some hope, though, when he informed me of a property management meet-up for Airbnb owners, where a group of Airbnb "super hosts" discussed ways to upscale and add more value or to find creative and innovative solutions for retaining their customers. Rentals were competitive and it was necessary for an entrepreneur to stay on their toes to get the desired effect.

Madelein started living with me and we were getting used to certain parts of our relationship, being more quarreled - more often - now. I felt like she wasn't home most days, and I would be out looking for business opportunities - so we could start building our Colombian roots. Priorities had to be set straight, and I needed to make money moves.

At the Airbnb property management meeting, I quickly realized this was closer to a band of fraternity brothers meeting for chapter. You really needed to have an "in," as this was an elite group of entrepreneurs and business owners. These men controlled all the properties and were seeking more things to own; and they were all Americans.

Having identified with the group, I also opened myself up to more opportunities. They were excited to meet someone willing to help found a startup, though some were skeptical of the industry being oversaturated. The fewer owners, the greater the returns for those already involved.

Three things mattered to me. One was the location - I didn't want to be in a place that exuded little life. Medellin was a beautiful place full of gorgeous, million-dollar views of the city. This was an environment where most people would give an arm or leg to get an apartment in, so they could be part of it. Airbnb owners declined requests from many tourists, so they could accommodate richer clients.

Second, the face of the property. I was very particular about what I had to give out. I had been in some types of houses and apartments, which were a mess from the jump. I had to decide whether what I might earn from renting to clients would be as tangible and heavenly as Provenza's atmosphere.

Lastly, I needed to decide if I could find someone credible to manage the property while I was away. Madelein was supportive, but I didn't want to encumber her with that.

I met a guy, named Mike, at the meeting. He was cheerful and was also a visionary, with many ideas for rental services. We shared some things in common. You know, the meeting was sort of a class-act, in the sense that we gathered at one of the fanciest restaurants in Provenza, which is surely done to ego-boost the gathering attendees.

After presenting some of my suggestions, the owners began to see I had something to offer. Mike asked me to meet at a club, later that night, so we could dig deeper into the future of rentals.

Attending the meet-up with the Airbnb group with my buddy Daniel helped me find my footing. Daniel was a "superhost" and ran Airbnb services, so I came with some connections myself. At first, the boys had not taken me seriously when I mentioned it, but bringing Daniel also made them see I was serious about starting up.

Mike loved to party. He was born in the United States, so we blended by virtue of my origins. At the club, he had his own space. A couple of girls sat around us, and he asked if I wanted any of them to accompany me. I humbly declined and asked him to get right to business.

**Mike:** You see Luke, most guys on the rental team are doing all they can to monopolize the business. What I suggest is that you look at other areas where you can come in. I can link you up with Javier. He is into another kind of service, but he is also a person of stature in the game.

I admired Mike because he was a man who made it easy to believe in a dream. He spoke so effortlessly about what the future of rental services would be like.

**Mike:** I intend to get some cars soon. With those cars, we can link up our Airbnb rentals with car-hailing services. What do you think?

I thought it was a good idea, but I was thinking of other things. Like, how long was it sustainable? The amount of maintenance and logistics - and the costs to pay for - such a project was going to add up fast.

One thing I loved about Mike was his ability to see opportunities everywhere. I learned details on the Airbnb services, and he fixed a date for another meeting with Daniel and me, so we could meet up with Javier. I was beginning to get acquainted with the Colombian air and people. The scent of Medellin and the innumerable sounds that rocked the streets. I was meant to be there. Our meeting was scheduled for the following week.

I had seen Javier briefly at the Airbnb meet-up. He wore a flannel shirt over a black pants and his brown boots were prominent. He had an air of composure about him that I liked from afar, so I was looking forward to meeting him further. He mentioned getting us setup with a helicopter flight to the Ultra rave, so I booked spots for six of us and felt great about the steps taking place.

When I got back home that night, the lights of the apartment were out, and I wondered what could have gone wrong. Could it have been a power surge? I went in, and to my surprise, Madelein had lit and linedup scented candles around the apartment, with flowers littered around. She was wearing red lingerie, and my head was swooning with the mixture of alcohol and giddiness, at the unexpected scene. Let's just say, that night was one of the best nights I have ever had with her.

The next morning, I woke up to find a note on the bed:

**Madelein:** Hey mi amor, I just want to thank you for your efforts. I see all that you do. I love you and I appreciate you. Kisses.

That morning, I stayed in bed a bit longer and I relived every bit of the moments and time with her. How did I come to this decision of wanting to start a life over in Colombia? Some months back, Colombia was just a place on the map - I had no affiliation to it. There wasn't anything leading me there, it was just a place that was meant to allow me to escape reality for a bit. I never envisioned that I would be planning a lifetime, with a partner, here. I found love. I had found a new path. I found a new life. I would give anything it took, to make it work.

The next Friday, Daniel and I met up with Mike and Javier at the club. Javier was looking animated, and he seemed to be engrossed with his phone as we spoke. He was also receiving calls a lot. When he eventually settled down and we exchanged pleasantries, we began to talk about real stuff, and I began to understand his actions.

Javier worked with a concierge service that catered to Airbnb clients and he told me how he helped clients get access to top restaurants and bars. Some of his clients were rich kids and celebrities who were hiding in Provenza to get away from the eyes of the media. He was well-known and he had a large network of people who worked as part of his service delivery team.

Javier and I clicked - we began to forge out ways we could make this project become a brand to be reckoned with. I told him I was going to create a website for my travel agency, The Luxour Experience. He was super supportive which gave me more inclination to get going. We were stoked for the upcoming Ultra festival the following day. Javier confirmed that I had six spots in the helicopter, and I needed to pick who was going. I had one more slot open as the current list was me, Madelein, Javier, Esteban, and Mike. Madelein had kept on talking about her best friend Vale, whom I had yet to meet, but that Vale's partner Brian was big into

74

crypto, a fellow American, and entrepreneur. She thought we would hit it off and be best friends. I asked for his number to give him a call and invite him. Unfortunately, I only had one more slot and he was going with Vale, so we made plans to meet in the VIP area at the festival.

The helicopter ride to Ultra was awesome and granted VIP access which allowed us entry into the common area for the DJs. Everyone there thought I was a DJ and kept asking for photos, which was a cool experience. Raves in Colombia are on another level. Madelein and I had so much fun until it started to rain uncontrollably. Brian and Vale met up with us in the VIP area and we hit it off. I could tell him, and I would be amazing friends. I was starting to feel confident thatI could live in Colombia comfortably, and make good quality friends that have the same drive to succeed as I had.

The next day, Madelein and I hung out with Daniel and his partner Karem. We discussed Ultra and wanted more cool experiences to do together. It turned out there was a Daddy Yankee show coming up which would be his last performance ever. On the spot, I purchased a box, or "balco" as they call it, for 10 people. Madelein was also a huge fan, so it was an easy sell.

At the Daddy Yankee concert, I pulled out my faux fur coats for everyone to wear. Our table was fun, and we all looked great. We went with Madelein, her aunt, Daniel, Kerem, and all our new friends. People thought we were famous and took a bunch of photos of us. I felt like I was living in a movie or a TV show. I felt like the esteemed Hollywood actor, Leonardo DiCaprio, with all the attention I was getting. After the concert, we went to a party at Nomad Finca, a breathtaking mansion in Envigado owned by Brian's roommate who was also named Brian. We called him Brian Nomad to differentiate the two more easily.

There is something about finding happiness in the middle of nowhere. You cling on to every moment because you know quite alright that, somewhere, there's a reality waiting for you when you back from that experience. I haven't always been one to place too much consciousness on events, but since my uncle's death, I have come to appreciate the gift of time - to see that time could be an ally and a foe. An ally to one who has truly lived, without holding back; and a foe to anyone who shrinks back at embracing life to the fullest.

The following day, we went to an entrepreneur meet-up at Oku's which was incredible. I loved talking to new people and networking with like-minded individuals. I met Robin, one of the owners of OKUS, and we hit it off. He called me his new brother and it meant the world to me. He ended up inviting me and my new friend Keesan, a crypto VC, to an exclusive event at the restaurant the next day. This was strictly a VIP event. I was beginning to meet some bigwigs in the money world of Medellin entrepreneurs, who also fancied the town for its vivaciousness.

This event was wild; it was an exclusive fashion event at the Okus Restaurant. I had my drone team come to get footage to document the awesome experience. Super good move on my part, as I was able to share it on Instagram, with Robin, and the SBQ owner Santiago to have for looking back on whenever we wanted.

I was having fun and loving the city - I was getting the recognition that I was also stoked to have new connections like both Brian's and Keesan, who had large portfolios and multiple businesses. My mind was beginning to expand at the endless possibilities that Medellin and Colombia had in store for me.

Life is one hell of an unpredictable journey. You seem to have it all figured out, and yet, you find yourself second-guessing even the surest of all decisions. There's a need to question our certainties, beliefs, and thoughts; and when we shy away from doing so, life brings circumstances that make us prove what we claim to believe in.

I was in love, but I knew love would not be enough to sustain us for the long run. Madelein was everything to me and Colombia had welcomed me graciously. It gave me meaning and an urgency of purpose.

It had been a while since I last spoke with my mom, so I called her. It takes a lot of courage to break from your parents' expectations - no matter how grown, they always see us as their babies.

My mom asked a variety of questions. Who was the new girl who Cayley told her about? What was I doing with my life? How is therapy? She hoped I was fine since the passing of my uncle. For mom, she felt a sense of ease if she were physically closer to me, but the years of distance taught her to become solid from afar too; and she learned to accept me for "my ways." I missed her presence, her fussing, her cooking. I knew she would see Madelein soon and I could barely wait for them to meet.

# The Journey to Forever

## Chapter Eight

---

M y time at the penthouse was coming to an end and I wanted to make my investment. I decided to purchase an apartment at Energy Living so that I could rent it out on Airbnb. I spent about $300k on the apartment and had $40k remaining. I moved that to an account, which Keesan's lawyer opened for me - that turned out to be a scam. I lost the money and was devastated. I didn't know what to do and went into a state of depression.

Therapy still worked and helped me get through everything. I didn't want more time to move on from my uncle's death, but I didn't want to go into details of other areas of my life. Eventually, I was returned from my leave of absence and continued working. Unfortunately, I was paycheck to paycheck as I tried figuring out my next steps, including how to support my lifestyle with Madelein.

I was living in two different countries, but it felt like I was taking a stroll in a town. Love has a way of giving us strength, and I started feeling assured in my decision about how to move forward.

Brian and I had forged a closer bond. It was also sweet that his partner Vale and Madelein got along well. We planned a trip to the Dominican Republic, a beautiful country with lovely waters. There are many places in the world that make one wonder how vast the universe is. For instance, we went on a trip to Guadalajara, Mexico for a rave called Wonderland with Madelein, Brian, Vale, Brian Nomad, and his girlfriend Evelyn. Mexico was my mother's home and it felt good to be there.

I loved Madelein and if I was making this much effort to be with her in Colombia, I expected that she would see things from a different light as well. With women, there is often a sense they deserve whatever it is that comes to them. Which, in most cases, is quite true, think about it - it takes a man who knows a woman's worth to go the extra mile. I knew her worth, and I was willing to give all it took.

Work began and being away from Madelein felt like torture. I became used to her being around, so it hurt that much more, being away from her. I had already left the mindset of working a regular job behind. In fact, the time I had in Medellin and having those business ideas planned made it seem like I was already my own boss.

Adjusting to a life without her constant presence was more challenging than I had anticipated. The routine I had come to cherish was abruptly interrupted, and I found myself grappling with a sense of emptiness. Every day without her felt like an unfulfilled promise, and the little moments we once shared seemed to magnify the distance between us. The small, everyday interactions that had become so familiar—her laughter, the way she would remind me of little things—were now starkly absent. I missed the simple pleasure of her company, the easy conversation, and the comfort of knowing she was just a touch away. This newfound absence forced me to confront how deeply she had become ingrained in my daily life, making her absence all the more poignant.

Admittedly, the distance added strain to our relationship. There were times I would go on work expeditions, which meant Madelein and I could not communicate for some time. She sometimes thought I took the trips intentionally or just said I was not able to talk, so I could have my own time or have time to be unfaithful. It made me laugh sometimes, but I felt her pain. We tasted what it felt like to be together and we were desperate to hold on to it forever.

My research into the gold industry was concrete, so I wanted to develop a pair of glasses equipped with a magnetic coupling idea I wanted to invent for a chain attachment. I began laying the groundwork for faux fur coats, jewelry, and other products that I intended to market and sell on the website INTERNATIONALGOLDEXPRESS.COM. I also built my travel agency website - LUXOUR.CO. Demand already existed to start capitalizing on, so I expanded on designing sunglasses, which I contracted help from a company in Los Angeles for.

Creating a brand that resonates with people who have a sense of class and adventure was something I was destined to do. Watching myself grow into this entrepreneur made me realize how far I have come. From a kid who was laughed at for wearing his hair the length of a girl's, to the boy who struggled with the separation of his parents. I was a young man seeking love from different people, but trying so hard to fit into my parents' idea of what was in store for me. Now, I was becoming the man who was finding his voice and bearing. It seemed like all my past experiences had been a rehearsal for what the future held.

I loved the idea of having to call the shots, but since I had lost a large chunk of change, I just needed to stay afloat. Working paycheck to paycheck would have to keep my head above water until everything in the works started to materialize.

I've been thinking about what happens to a love that shatters, a love that dies before its root is perpetually enshrined in the ground. People deal differently with heartbreak, and I came to Colombia to escape from the memory of being hurt myself. I found Madelein, and yes, we have had our issues and days where love may feel so hard. What is love without a test of what we really feel, though?

It's easy to say we love someone, it's easy to claim that we want forever with a person. When push comes to shove, every intention is revealed.

LUXOUR.CO is going to blow the minds of customers when we start rolling out our packages and I couldn't wait to see the International Gold Express (IGE) sunglasses being showcased across stores and online.

Expanding to a clothing line is something else I have considered, and decided to pursue later - the world is a vast place with endless possibilities. As I dig deeper, maybe I'll begin to find new territories to conquer.

Starting from scratch all over and building my dreams was a Herculean task. If I had known that things would be this tough, I could have changed my mind. I was shuttling between America and Colombia to manage the apartment I bought, but my bills and tax payments were also piling up. Regardless, I had to pursue other areas of development, and slowly but surely, pushed all my projects along.

Madelein was a lady with a taste for the finest things of life and I was always determined to please her. I had to make her happy because if I did not, it was going to seem like I was all talk and no action. I assured her of my capability to meet her needs, but candidly, it was strenuous having to balance it all.

One of the setbacks of working and building a vision at the same time is that you cannot always tell where and when your gaze might become hazy.

For instance, if I had to physically be on-site for my job in the United States, which took up all my time. When I finished my long workday, I didn't go out to see friends; instead, I worked on product designs or pushed along my website for the travel agency. I was determined to build a profitable company, but how would I balance things up? A clash of interest is sure to make one lose track of where they need to concentrate their energy, you know.

Overall, I was motivated by the fact I knew all of this was temporary, and soon the financial freedom I craved would come. I have been able to get this far by having a good network of guys who share the same vision as me. One of new my best friends - and current business partner - Brian always told me:

**Brian:** You are a product of your environment.

I also believe it's important to have a community of like minds who help us stay focused when things are not going as planned. Madelein understood it would be difficult to meet *all* her demands, but she also knew I wasn't the sort of man to refuse her or hold back in my display of affection for her - that I genuinely love her.

I could sense her frustration the first time I looked at her and said:

**Luke:** Baby, we cannot afford the bill for that party right now.

I felt bad for her, but there was nothing I could do about it. My priority needed to be ensuring the smooth running of our income operations, even if it meant having to cut back on certain luxuries. Besides, we had a lot of memories to draw from.

Eventually, our trips and travels became less frequent, as I wanted them to be when starting to look towards the bigger picture. Being away from Madelein felt like losing a part of myself. I wanted to be with her all the time, but we had to make do with the current arrangement. Loving Madelein was a gift that I cherished for several reasons.

There was the part of discovering myself. Having to find that I was just living a life without any soul. There was no aim to my pursuit all these years, beyond living for the rat race or going through the motions. She opened my eyes to parts of me that were hidden, undiscovered. Since meeting Madelein, one truth has always been certain - I've never been more focused in my life. I guess that's what made, and continues to make, her stand out.

I do not want a future, or a life without her. Rather, I want to exist where I am assured someone else is there, who understands all the parts of me that I am unwilling to open up to anyone else.

The first time I knew I was going to marry Madelein was on a windy afternoon when spring was beginning to bloom in the hearts of the plants and flowers. Medellin was blossoming and I loved the verdant splendor of the city.

We went to the park but got a bit bored, so we went sightseeing for a change of scenery. She was wearing a floral gown and her hair loosely. As she moved in the wind, I wondered if I had ever seen someone so beautiful.

My first attraction to Madelein was her ability to brainstorm with me. She was not just beautiful; she was also smart and affable. When we were sitting on the park bench, she said to me:

**Madelein:** Why are you staring at me like that?

I had so much to say to her.

I wanted to tell her that she was a new beginning for me. I wanted her to see that she was the woman who made me become a man in more ways than I could have imagined. She was my joy in the sad times and my light in the dark times - particularly, when I was fighting to understand my uncle's demise.

In February 2023, I decided to visit Madelein for my birthday trip but wanted this one to be different. I thought the best way to celebrate would be with Madelein, in Mexico, to meet my mom and sister. I could fly her out and I was giddy at the idea since her meeting my mom was important to me.

Madelein quickly made an impression on my mom *and* Cayley. It was sweet watching them get along.

Cayley began to see that I was serious about her. From the onset, she had her reservations, but seeing what we had become, she began to see that maybe there was something substantial to what we felt. I would have loved to stay longer in Mexico, but also felt the need to catch up with work.

Back in the States, I began to think of creative ways to propose to Madelein. I thought about taking her to the islands, but it also felt banal, and I decided to do something unique.

We planned for a short getaway to Guatape and I was in contact with my drone crew who made videos and content for my travel brand. The idea was to make an epic proposal that would make any woman's dream, and I could promote wedding and proposal events. I thought making amazing content would help my travel and lifestyle brand, LUXOUR.CO, and show the world I can create extraordinary experiences for them. Little did I know that this reel would help me get cast on reality television later.

We booked a mansion for the weekend, and all was set. A famous Colombian soccer player named James Rodríguezowned the house. I scheduled a helicopter to fly over and drop purple smoke, while I proposed, and then circle back to pick us up for a brief celebratory helicopter ride. I had the drone crew on standby to capture footage. Chris, Brian, Ashley, Vale, and others were all there to celebrate with us. Chris and Ashley were another couple Madelein and I got along with. I could already tell that Chris and I would be great friends for the rest of our lives. We had planned a yacht party the following day and another party at the house afterwards.

The morning of the proposal, Madelein woke up and coordinated her outing with the camera crew, while I already arranged for the other content to be recorded and staged in the best manner possible. The proposal was amazing, and I was so stoked that Madelein accepted. When I got on my knees to ask her to marry me, something unexpected happened. I said:

**Luke:** Baby, I knew from the moment I met you that I wanted to spend the rest of my life with you. You're the most beautiful woman I know, and I can't imagine a life without you by my side. You're my best friend and partner and I want to make you my wife. Will you marry me?

She looked at me and smiled but didn't say anything for a full eight seconds. I didn't know what to do, it felt like a lifetime. Supposedly, she was in shock, but finally managed to say "yes." She gave me her wrong hand, the right hand, to put the ring on - which makes for a funny memory, looking back. Regardless, she said "yes," and we were finally engaged!

After the proposal, I went back to the States. Robert was out of town for a while and decided to come see me. We hung out at our usual spot, the same place where it all began. Our Colombian bartender no longer worked at the bar, but I wanted to thank him for inspiring the move to Colombia and to tell him I had found the greatest love of my life. Wherever he is, I hope he finds what he's looking for too. We were hoping Zach would join us, but dude was too busy to make time for us. After a couple of drinks, Robert asked:

**Robert:** Dude, you really want to marry this girl?

He had never been excited about the idea of finding the love of my life on Instagram. It's interesting that I was initially the skeptical one, and now, he had doubts regarding the validity of our love.

**Luke:** Listen, man, I have never been more certain about anything in my life.

He gave a big grin.

**Robert:** You are so confident you are willing to change your life for her sake and that's what bothers me. This chick has a good grip on you man.

I came too far to even listen to my doubting thoughts. You know those thoughts that creep in, during moments when you and your partner are trying to patch things up, but it was too late to turn back now.

In July 2023, we partied in Guatape for Madelein's 19th birthday. For some reason, she wasn't keen on spending that time with me in Medellin. I felt she just needed a change of scenery, but I wasn't able to afford such a trip, so we had to stall. I noticed she was somewhat edgy with me. Let's just say, we had a blowout fight, and I left Medellin on bad terms with Madelein.

We were not on the best talking terms when I got back to the States. Shortly after I returned, I heard a rumor about infidelity.

I was looking for clues to determine if there was any truth to the rumors, as I did not want to build my relationship on assumptions, despite knowing Madelein was popular. It was a big deal, if the rumors were true, because we had just gotten engaged. It didn't make sense.

What bothered me the most was the way we were losing communication. Madelein had always been expressive about her feelings and desires, but we were talking less in the few days I had come home.

What is a long-distance relationship without trust? If I was going to stay in a relationship, I needed to be honest with myself that it wouldn't always be smooth sailing.

I began to ask her questions and she got pissed that I was choosing the rumors over her. These were not questions I wanted to ask, but I had drawn a line of what to expect. Truth be told, I wasn't prepared for the news of cheating, especially being so far away from her when finding out. If it were true, I know I would find it difficult to let go.

I flew back on September 2nd to celebrate our one-year anniversary and figure out what the heck happened. She confirmed things being said were just made up.

It's true, what they say, about a love that grows cold - it withers away when it is not given the nurturing and nourishment it needs for life. What do we say when love burns and consumes us with terror? I was missing her, the Madelein I felt was no longer the person I was seeing. I was seeing someone different. What had become of the future we had planned for?

Every major business decision I had taken in the past couple of months was motivated by her. I considered changing my plans and leaving the businesses behind. The thought of letting the woman I had come to admire, so dearly, was something I could not let slip out of my palms.

What was love, without some hope of forever? What was love, without a fight or two? Madelein was my destination, and I wasn't going to let her go. I was holding onto the memories we had shared and the things we had promised each other. I had come too far to let it all go. I, we, had come too far to not try and make this work. It was great we both agreed on that and were invested in the longevity of the relationship, but it made having to go home that much harder.

Back in the States, it became obvious I wasn't going to be at peace with the way things were. Madelein became a huge part of my life and I felt like I was choking, that I needed air, being away from her - it was a torrential hurt.

Remember when I spoke about being hurt in the balls earlier on in this story? I compared that to my uncle's death, as well as the months of torture during my fights with Madelein. I think what made my separation from Madelein hurt more than anything else, was that while my uncle's death was final and settled, being at a distance from Madelein was a painful uncertainty that bothered me beyond all hope. I needed to make a change.

Love is a battlefield. Love is a journey that reveals all intentions. Above all, love is a decision that you mustgive it all you've got, against all odds, to make it work.

**Luke:** My sweet Madelein, I thought I had a life before I met you. I never knew I was just existing. I thought I had a meaning, before meeting you, but I never knew I was just a speck in the universe. Right now, you may not believe me, but if my heart could speak, it would say, "You and me forever."

As far as what is next for us, we have the businesses to focus on and continue growing. Our social media, websites, and other platforms are ways you can keep up with us and see how our story unfolds.

Who knows, maybe another story about "Maintaining Madelein," could be next? She is my everything and I hope you continue supporting our journey together.

# About the Author

Luke Berry, author of Meeting Madelein, gained widespread attention for his compelling journey on a reality TV show, where viewers were captivated by his quest for a happy ending. A first-generation American with degrees in mining engineering, geology, and an MBA, Luke has channeled his diverse expertise into several ventures. He founded The Luxour Experience, a premier travel agency, and International Gold Express, a high-end jewelry and sunglasses company.

Passionate about inspiring others to seek a better life, Luke's career reflects his commitment to excellence and innovation. When he's not writing or managing his businesses, he shares his adventures on Instagram (@dom.berry.on). Luke divides his time between Los Angeles and Medellin, pursuing his dreams and encouraging others to follow their own.

Milton Keynes UK
Ingram Content Group UK Ltd.
UKHW051139100924
448143UK00018B/187